Creative Projects
with Raspberry Pi

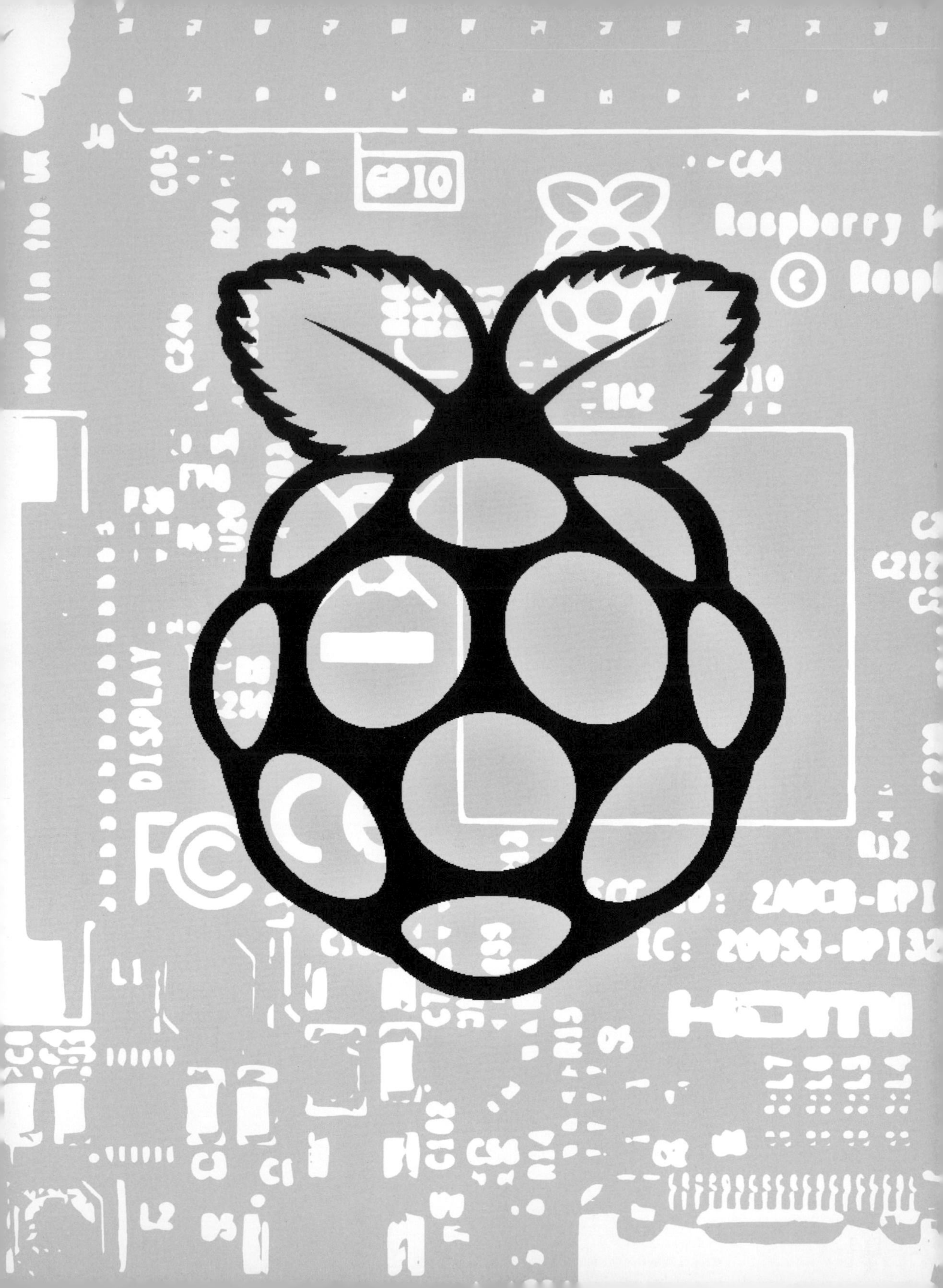
DISPLAY
HDMI

Creative Projects
with Raspberry Pi

Build gadgets, cameras, tools, home automation, games, and more

Kirsten Kearney and **Will Freeman**

Foreword by David Braben OBE FREng, co-founder of the Raspberry Pi Foundation

Abrams Image, New York

Raspberry Pi is a trademark of the Raspberry Pi Foundation,
which does not sponsor, authorize, or endorse this book.

Creative Projects with Raspberry Pi

Library of Congress Control Number: 2016912032

ISBN: 978-1-4197-2500-5

This book was conceived, designed, and produced by:
Quintet Publishing Limited
4th Floor, Ovest House
58 West Street
Brighton BN1 2RA
United Kingdom

Printed and bound in China

10 9 8 7 6 5 4 3 2 1

Abrams Image books are available at special discounts when purchased
in quantity for premiums and promotions as well as fundraising or
educational use. Special editions can also be created to specification.
For details, contact specialsales@abramsbooks.com or the address below.

 ABRAMS
The Art of Books

115 West 18th Street
New York, NY 10011
abramsbooks.com

Contents

Foreword

It is fantastic to see the many diverse projects that have been brought to life since the first Raspberry Pi came out. To me it is reminiscent of the creative spirit of the 1980s, when many people's computers did not have screws in their lids (if they had lids fitted at all), and frequently had wires or ribbon cable and bits of badly soldered Veroboard covered in components hanging out of them. This was the spirit of experimentation; of modifying and improving things so they could do special or unusual tasks that the basic computer couldn't manage (or at least couldn't perform as quickly). The key thing about this spirit is that with it came a "familiarity"—there was an understanding of how the computers worked.

For me, the Raspberry Pi story began around 2003, when I noticed a sharp decrease in the number of graduate applicants to Frontier Developments plc. (where my "day job" is CEO). It turned out that it was a much wider problem, especially for universities running Computer Science courses, where enrollment had dropped off very badly. The big question was "Why?"

At Frontier we were making games with Sony, Aardman Animations, and Atari, and one of the questions we asked focus test members was "What is your most boring subject at school?" Shockingly the most common answer was "ICT" (Information and Communication Technology), a then-new subject in British schools that had replaced Computer Science. While Computer Science included robots, soldering, and all the great things you will find in this book, ICT was mostly based on the non-technical teaching of office skills, which was seen as deathly dull.

< 6 >

With the problem identified, a key part of the solution was to find a way to teach Computer Science to people. Raspberry Pi was founded by six of us from both Cambridge University and from industry, all coming at the problem in slightly different ways, but sharing a common goal. Winding forward to today, we now have sold over 12.5 million Raspberry Pis (at time of writing), Computer Science is back in UK schools, and programming is fashionable again.

It is great to see the faces of kids and adults who have made something themselves. There have been many great projects—both personal and within clubs—that have ranged from making an LED blink to running a program on the International Space Station. The confidence these projects give the person (or people) behind them is great to see: techno-fear ebbs away and is replaced by an ambition to do something even better.

Looking through this book, it is amazing to see the things people have done with a Pi, and I hope you are inspired to do something equally amazing yourself!

David Braben OBE FREng
Raspberry Pi Foundation co-founder
CEO Frontier Developments plc

< 7 >

Introduction

In the modern age we use numerous technologies to understand and connect with the world around us: computers, smart devices, and a variety of other gadgets. Yet while we know how to use our tech to simplify the world around us, most of us don't know how to make these items, or how to create the programs that control them. In other words, when it comes to technology, we can all "read," but we can't all "write."

Raspberry Pi changes all of that. This little computer is not only cheap, flexible, and accessible, but it is supported by a worldwide community that is passionate about sharing its ideas, experiences, and skills. For children and adults of all abilities it is the ideal platform to learn more about electronics, engineering, and programming—to learn to write with our technology, rather than just reading from it.

Starting with a simple Raspberry Pi project, you will quickly see how anybody can take control of technology. The Raspberry Pi will help push you in the right direction, support you as you tackle more complex challenges, and—if you desire—lead you to mastering more advanced technologies. A Raspberry Pi is much more than a beginner's tool, though, and in the pages of this book you will see a range of Pi projects that vary in scale and ambition.

Working with a Pi is about stretching your capabilities, your understanding, and even challenging your own self-belief as you attempt to create things that you perhaps felt were beyond your limits. With that in mind, we've written this book to inspire you, teach you, and help you become a Raspberry Pi expert. We hope you enjoy learning what's possible with this tiny computer, and remember—there's no reason why you can't be the master of the technology you use!

Kirsten & Will

< 8 >

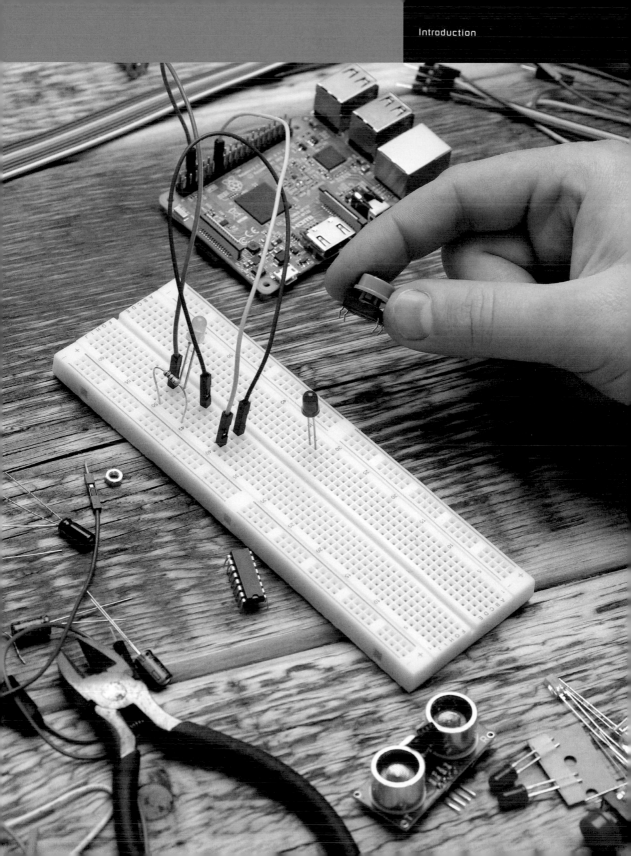

Pi Projects

Key

■ THE BASIC PI-DEA

■ ROBOT PI

■ GAME PI

■ EXPERIMENTAL PI

■ HOME PI

■ ART PI

Blinking LED page 40

Shutdown Button page 44

PiNoculars page 50

RoboCroc page 54

CamTank page 58

Raspberry Pi HAL 9000 page 64

Box Bot page 68

PIK3A Retro Gaming Table page 76

< 10 >

The code for all the projects marked "Build it!" can be found at:
quartoknows.com/page/raspberry-pi See page 9 for more details.

Micro Arcade Cabinet page 82

$20 Portable Games Console page 86

Meccano Rubik's Shrine page 90

Retro Games Station page 96

Robust Minecraft® Server page 100

Batinator page 106

SoilCam page 110

GroveWeatherPi page 114

Astro Pi page 120

< 11 >

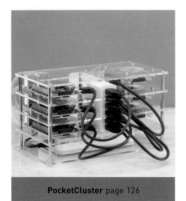

PocketCluster page 126

Build it!

Sensor Station page 130

Movie Player page 136

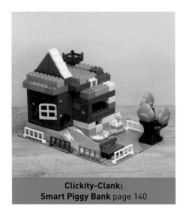

**Clickity-Clank:
Smart Piggy Bank** page 140

Internet Monitor page 144

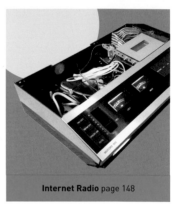

Internet Radio page 148

Coffee Roaster page 152

Cyberdeck page 158

Tytelli Smartphone page 162

< 12 >

Media Center page 166

Lunchbox Laptop page 172

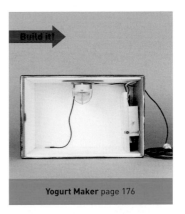

Yogurt Maker page 176

The Internet Of LEGO® page 184

3D Scanner page 192

BeetBox page 198

Erica The Cyber Rhino page 202

Pi Camera page 208

LEGO® Technic Case page 212

< 13 >

1

THE BASIC PI-DEA
An essential introduction to the Raspberry Pi

The History Of Raspberry Pi

Although the first Raspberry Pi hit the market in 2012, its history began in 1981, when the world was on the cusp of a microcomputer revolution.

In the early 1980s, the British Broadcasting Corporation—the UK's publicly funded TV broadcaster—launched its BBC Computer Literacy Project, which led to the development of the BBC Micro computer. With the UK government subsidizing half its cost, this platform quickly found its way into schools and other educational facilities; in the years that followed it successfully grew a generation of computer developers and engineers.

This growth didn't last, though. Between the mid 1990s and mid 2000s, one of these early computer engineers, Eben Upton, noticed a huge decline in the number of applicants for university places in computer science. Not only that, but the *quality* of the applicants had also declined, so while students knew how to use applications, they didn't know how to program to start with. Upton felt this heralded a crisis in the British technology industry: computer literacy was dying.

Upton's experience convinced him that the best way to increase the number of programmers and engineers—and therefore the amount of useful technology being created in the future—was to grow engineers from childhood, by putting the technology in their hands as soon as they were big enough to hold it. What he needed was to "reinvent" the BBC Micro for the 21st century.

This wasn't something he could do alone, though, and for six years he worked with colleagues, computer enthusiasts, teachers, and academics to create a platform that met an array of technical and philosophical criteria.

The team—which saw Upton joined by David Braben, Jack Lang, Pete Lomas, Alan Mycroft, and Robert Mullins—felt that digital technology was increasingly moving in a direction that encouraged consumption more than creation. They felt they needed to redress the balance and help the next generation become makers, enabling them to shape the world by creating their own technologies.

The microcomputer they needed would have to combine low cost with high performance. It needed to be physically small, have a video core, the ability to run 3D graphics, a keyboard interface, an SD card file system, and support a range of other devices. Over time, the team realized the computer would also need to offer a variety of programming languages, and host a suite of free, open-source software that would make it accessible, cross-disciplinary, and exciting for young people.

When the development team was looking to name its new platform, "Raspberry" was suggested (following other manufacturers' success with fruit-based names). As the plan

< 16 >

Less than three months after its launch, 4000 Raspberry Pi units were being manufactured every day to keep up with demand.

was for the machine to run Python, this expanded to "Raspberry Pi." The name stuck and the Raspberry Pi Foundation was registered in 2009, establishing a charity that would produce and supply the cheap, single-board, tiny computers. By 2012 the first versions of the Pi were ready and launched as the Model A and Model B in homage to the original models of the BBC Micro.

Despite plenty of initial interest, the team still had quite low expectations when it came to early commercial sales. It needn't have worried though, as the initial run of 10,000 boards sold out within minutes, with hundreds of thousands of preorders.

By May 2012—just three months after its launch—20,000 Raspberry Pis had been shipped. Less than five years on, sales hit 10 million units in September 2016, and they continue to climb as new generations start to explore one of the 21st century's greatest computing success stories.

The story of the Raspberry Pi can be traced back to the humble BBC Micro computer from the early 1980s.

< 17 >

Equipment

Raspberry Pi

Since the Raspberry Pi launched in 2012 there have been several models, including the Raspberry Pi Model A (and A+), Model B (and B+), and Raspberry Pi 2. The makers featured in this book have used a variety of models for their projects and the great thing is that they are often interchangeable.

Today, you are most likely to find people using the Raspberry Pi 3, which launched in 2016. The Pi 3 is easy to find, affordable, and compatible with both the Pi 1 and Pi 2 models. Unlike its predecessors, it also features built-in Wi-Fi and Bluetooth.

If size and/or power consumption is a major consideration for your project, then you may find you are better served by a Pi Zero. This is essentially a pared-down version of the "full size" Pi that loses a number of connection options and a little bit of performance.

However, its diminutive size makes it much easier to tuck into cramped projects, such as the $20 Portable Games Console on pages 86–89. The latest Pi Zero model (the Pi Zero W, launched in 2017) adds Wi-Fi and Bluetooth connectivity, making it the most versatile Pi Zero to date.

The selection of Pi models shows how the board has evolved since it first appeared in 2012.

1 Raspberry Pi Model B (2012)
2 Raspberry Pi Model A+ (2014)
3 Raspberry Pi Model B+ (2014)
4 Rasberry Pi 2 Model B (2015)
5 Raspberry Pi Zero ver. 1.3 (2015)
6 Raspberry Pi 3 model B (2016)
7 Raspberry Pi Zero W (2017)

< 18 >

Essential Accessories

On its own, a Raspberry Pi won't get you too far—you need some basic accessories to turn your small slab of circuitry and chips into a fully fledged computer. Fortunately, everything you need is commonplace, and you may find you already have much of what you need. Failing that, Raspberry Pis are often sold as kits, with all the extras, so you can get started straight away. But what exactly do you need?

A monitor or television is essential, so you can see what you're doing. You'll also need an HDMI cable to connect your Raspberry Pi to your screen.

You'll need a **mouse** and **keyboard** to operate your Pi: you can use USB or wireless versions, but cabled USB devices are easiest to start with.

An **SD memory card** is needed to store files and software on your Pi, as well as the operating system. Early Pi models used full-sized SD cards, but newer versions use a micro SD card. Either way, it's recommended that your card has a capacity of at least 8GB (gigabytes).

A **5V, 1A micro USB power supply** will work with all models of Raspberry Pi.

< 19 >

Optional Extras

An ever-increasing number of companies make special add-on extras to grant your Raspberry Pi new abilities. The Raspberry Pi Foundation's official accessories (shown here) are well supported, with plenty of information and helpful tips online. They are also very reliable and are common to many projects, including many of those that appear in this book.

The latest official **camera module** (v2 at the time of writing) can capture 8-megapixel still images and record high-definition video. Its simplicity, power, and flexibility have made it a stalwart of many of the most amazing Pi projects there are. It is also fully compatible with the Raspberry Pi 1, 2, and 3 models. You can see how to get your camera module up and running on pages 208–211, while the CamTank project on pages 58–63 shows how it can be taken a step further.

Sure, you don't need a **Raspberry Pi case**, but it will keep your Raspberry Pi safe and dust free. It can also make it easier to build the computer into your projects.

Unless you're using a Raspberry Pi 3, you'll need a Wi-Fi dongle to give it wireless connectivity. There are countless wireless connection options available, but the official **Raspberry Pi USB Wi-Fi dongle** is guaranteed to be compatible with your Pi.

< 20 >

The **Raspberry Pi touch display** is a 7-inch touchscreen monitor that can help transform your Raspberry Pi into a laptop or entertainment hub, such as the Movie Player on pages 136–139. The screen comes with an adaptor board to connect to your Pi, and is very simple to hook up.

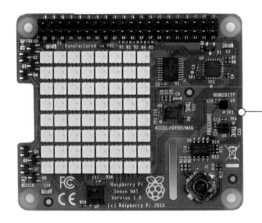

The **Sense HAT** was designed for the Astro Pi space mission featured on pages 120–125, and now it's available to everyone. It provides your Raspberry Pi with a tiny joystick controller, an LED display, and an array of sensors that add a gyroscope, accelerometer, magnetometer, barometric pressure detector, and humidity and temperature readers. You can build your own Sense HAT-based Sensor Station by following the instructions on pages 130–133.

Unlike the standard Pi camera module, the **Pi NoIR camera module** isn't fitted with an infrared (IR) filter. This means that it can record "invisible" IR wavelengths, enabling it to see in the dark. For certain projects, such as the Batinator on pages 106–109, being able to take clear images in the dead of night is essential.

< 21 >

Workbench Tools

As your Raspberry Pi projects move beyond the board itself you will find that you need a variety of electronics tools and equipment. Although it's impossible to know for sure what you will need for each and every project you undertake, there are several items that you will find yourself reaching for with regularity.

A **solder-less breadboard** lets you prototype circuits without soldering, so you can move things around until everything works. You'll also need some **jump wires**, which can be plugged into your breadboard's holes.

A basic electronics toolkit should include **electronics screwdrivers**, **precision tweezers**, **crimping pliers**, and **wire cutters**. It won't be necessary for your first projects, but as you become more ambitious these items can prove invaluable.

< 22 >

When it comes to connecting wires and circuit boards a **soldering iron** is essential. You will also need some solder, a stand, a wet sponge to keep things clean, and flux (unless you are using "flux-core" solder, which contains flux).

A supply of **wire** in different colors and gauges will help you build circuits for your projects. The gauge (or thickness) of the wire determines the current it can carry.

Your local electronics store will likely sell a components selection pack containing **LEDs**, **resistors**, **diodes**, and many other useful parts. It's worth having spares as you experiment, as you will almost inevitably make mistakes along the way.

A **multimeter** enables you to measure the voltage, current, and resistance in a circuit, helping you to locate (and avoid) faults in your circuits.

< 23 >

Jargon Buster

If you're new to Raspberry Pi you will undoubtedly encounter some words, phrases, and acronyms that leave you scratching your head. This quick guide will help you understand some of the most important terms you should know.

GPIO

As you read through this book you'll see "GPIO" mentioned a lot of the time. This stands for "General Purpose Input Output." If you take a look at a Raspberry Pi (1, 2, or 3), you can see a small grid of pins sticking out of the top (shown below). Those are programmable GPIO pins that can be used to connect devices and extra parts to your Raspberry Pi.

On a Pi Zero, the GPIO is "unpopulated," which means there are no pins. You can, however, add a GPIO header by buying one and soldering it in, or simply solder wires directly to the GPIO pads on the board.

Code

Code is a written language that computers can understand. When you write code, computers

can read it. You can use code to control your Raspberry Pi, change the way it works, or even create your own software that will run on your tiny computer. The projects in this book use code to let their various parts work together, and with a little time and effort, you'll find that you can write in code as if it were your own language. There are many different types of coding languages.

The Raspberry Pi 3 (below top) has 40 GPIO pins that you can solder and connect to. However, a Pi Zero's GPIO (below bottom) is "unpopulated" to keep the board's size to a minimum.

< 24 >

Internet of Things (IoT)

The "Internet of Things" refers to the network of millions of physical objects linked up by the Internet. We're not just talking about computers here, but watches, games consoles, security cameras, medical equipment, and even whole buildings. Whether their builder intends it or not, countless Raspberry Pi-powered projects join the IoT, as most of them are "things," with a Raspberry Pi connecting them to the world through the Internet.

Maker

In the world of computing, hacking, and electronics, "maker" has come to refer to anybody who likes to build and create. These people are often amateurs, typically like to improvise as they go, and more often than not prefer to build things themselves rather than buying them ready made. Every project in this book is the creation of a maker.

The Internet of LEGO® on pages 184–191 provides a small-scale demonstration of the Internet of Things.

Operating System

On its own, computer hardware isn't much use to humans. For us to be able to use it— and make things for it—it needs an operating system (like Windows, macOS, or Linux). All the applications that run on a computer use its operating system, and so do many of the devices you attach to it. We use the operating system (also known as an "OS") when we interact with tools such as the computer's home screen or a mouse cursor. On a Raspberry Pi, the operating system is known as "Raspbian."

< 25 >

Python

Raspberry Pis can read all sorts of different types of code (also known as "languages"), but the most common by far is Python. Python is easy to learn, quick to use, and is recommended by the Raspberry Pi Foundation as the best option for most learners. You can read more about the basics of code on pages 37–39.

Raspbian

Raspbian is the standard operating system for Raspberry Pi, which is built on the free, Linux-based Debian OS. Raspbian provides the basic programs and utilities that let your Raspberry Pi run, and enables you to create brilliant projects. Other operating systems can be installed on the Pi, but if you start out with Raspbian, you'll find it easier to learn the basics, build your first projects, and make use of lots of software created by other people who use Raspbian.

Scratch

Scratch is a basic programming language aimed primarily at introducing computer code to younger audiences thanks to its easy-to-use, "drag-and-drop" interface. This makes it ideal for teaching scenarios, but it does have its limitations. This is why more experienced builders prefer to use Python or one of many other languages.

Erica The Cyber Rhino uses code written in Python, as well as other languages. You can find out more about Erica on pages 202–207.

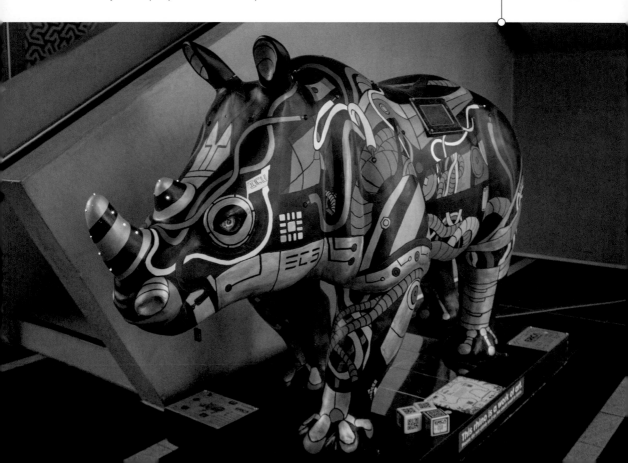

Resistors are color-coded to indicate their resistance. It's worth familiarizing yourself with this coding system so you can quickly tell if you're using the correct item or not.

Color	Value	Multiplier	Tolerance
Black	0	x1	
Brown	1	x10	1%
Red	2	x100	2%
Orange	3	x1K	–
Yellow	4	x10K	–
Green	5	x100K	0.5%
Blue	6	x1M	0.25%
Violet	7	x10M	0.1%
Gray	8	–	0.05%
White	9	–	–
Gold	–	0.1	5%
Silver	–	0.01	10%

Resistors

Resistors are one of the most commonly used components in electronic circuits. In Raspberry Pi projects they are often used to limit the electrical current flowing around a circuit, which is particularly useful when it comes to powering LEDs. You can see examples of resistors in action in the Blinking LED and Yogurt Maker projects, which you'll find on pages 40–43 and 176–181 respectively.

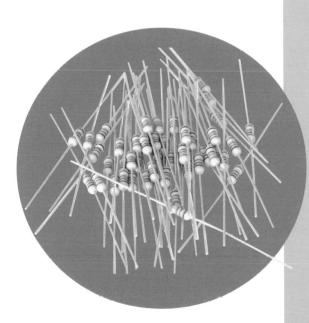

First Color	Third Color
First figure	Multiplier

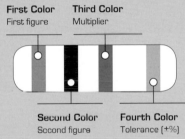

Second Color	Fourth Color
Second figure	Tolerance (±%)

The color code indicates the resistance. In the example above, the colors are brown (1), black (0), orange (x1K), and gold (±5%). Put this together and you can tell that the resistance is 10 x 1K, or 10,000 Ohms, with a tolerance of ±5%.

The resistor shown below has two red bands, followed by brown and gold. Again, we can "read" the colors to determine the resistance. In this case, the first three values are 2, 2, and x10, which tells us this is a 220 Ohm resistor (22 x 10). The gold again indicates a tolerance of ±5%.

< 27 >

Getting Started

If you've never used (or seen) a Raspberry Pi before, the bare board can seem slightly daunting. This simple guide will walk you through everything you need to do to get started.

Exploring Your Raspberry Pi

Before we get into the nitty gritty details of setting up the Raspberry Pi, let's be clear on what it actually is. A Raspberry Pi is a Linux-based, single-board computer in a small form factor. It is not only capable of fast data processing, but is also able to interact with the physical world through its various inputs and outputs that can include USB, HDMI, Ethernet, and built-in Wi-Fi (depending on the model you choose).

Raspberry Pi Zero W
SPECIFICATION

> 1Ghz single-core CPU
> 512MB RAM
> Micro USB data port
> Micro USB power port
> Mini HDMI port
> Micro SD card slot
> Unpopulated 40-pin GPIO header
> 802.11n Wireless LAN
> Bluetooth
> Size: 2.6" × 1.2" × 0.2"

< 28 >

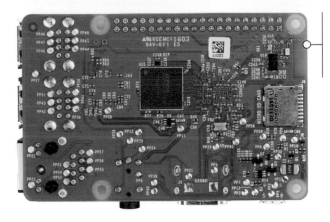

The small-format Raspberry Pi 3 is perfect for building into your projects, although if space is at a premium you can always use a Pi Zero (shown opposite) instead.

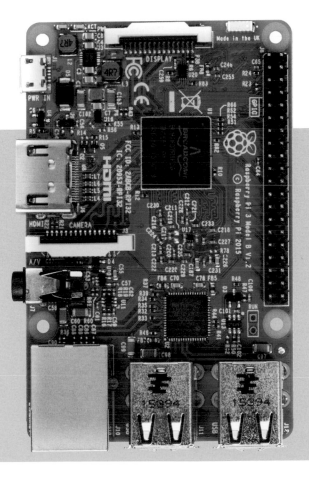

Raspberry Pi 3 Model B
SPECIFICATION

> 1.2GHz 64-bit quad-core CPU

> 1GB RAM

> 802.11n Wireless LAN

> Bluetooth

> 4 full-sized USB ports

> Full-sized HDMI port

> Ethernet port

> Combined 3.5mm audio jack and composite video

> Micro SD card slot

> VideoCore IV 3D graphics

> 40 GPIO pins

> Size: 3.4" × 2.2" (height determined by connectors)

< 29 >

Anatomy Of The Pi 3

The **GPIO connector** is a male header that can be used to interface various pieces of hardware with the Raspberry Pi. The Raspberry Pi 3 has 40 GPIO pins, which can handle small currents of up to 3.3V.

The **display port** is a ribbon connector port used to connect the Pi to its dedicated LCD display.

On the underside of the Raspberry Pi is a **micro SD card slot** for the memory card that contains the Pi's operating system, software, and other files.

The Raspberry Pi is powered by a **5V micro USB adaptor.** You can buy a dedicated power supply or use a smartphone charger (rated at least 1A for smooth performance).

The **HDMI port** is used to connect the Raspberry Pi to a display.

< 30 >

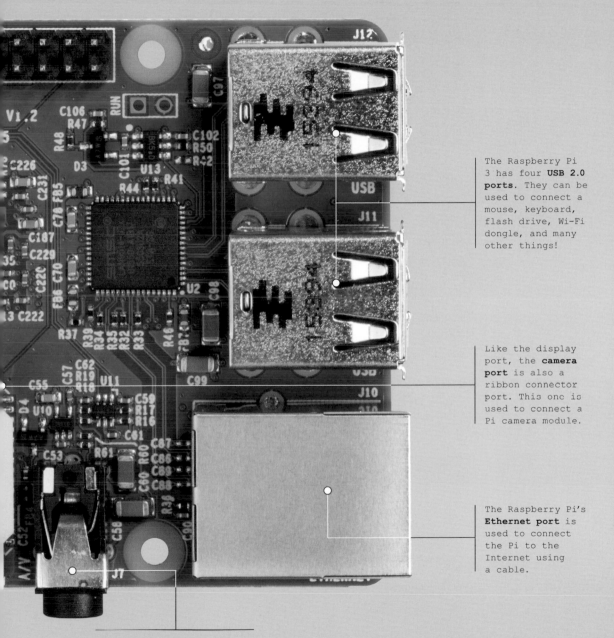

The Raspberry Pi 3 has four **USB 2.0 ports.** They can be used to connect a mouse, keyboard, flash drive, Wi-Fi dongle, and many other things!

Like the display port, the **camera port** is also a ribbon connector port. This one is used to connect a Pi camera module.

The Raspberry Pi's **Ethernet port** is used to connect the Pi to the Internet using a cable.

The **composite video jack** is used to connect the Pi to a composite video display. It requires some configuration to get it started.

< 31 >

Cases

Once you start connecting the various cables to your Raspberry Pi, it can become hard to keep the board in one place, and easy to damage it accidentally. This can be frustrating, so before you start to work with it, it's a good idea to put your Pi in a case. Many of the projects in this book benefit from having the board in some sort of enclosure.

If you want to make your own, you can find instructions for building one out of LEGO® on pages 212–215. Alternatively, you can simply attach your Raspberry Pi to an acrylic base, as described below, which will allow it to "float" safely above your desktop rather than sitting on top of it.

MATERIALS

→ Piece of acrylic
(approx. 6" x 6")

→ 4 x M2.5 x 25mm screws

→ 12 x M2.5 nuts

1. Take your piece of acrylic and place the Raspberry Pi at its center.

2. Mark the Pi's four (yellow) mounting holes on the acrylic and drill them using a suitable drill bit.

3. Push a bolt through each of the four holes and tighten a nut onto each of them.

4. Add another nut to each bolt, but only screw it a short way down the bolt.

5. Sit your Raspberry Pi on the nuts you added in the previous step and use your final four nuts to clamp the board in place. Take care not to overtighten the bolts.

Preparing NOOBS

The next stage is to prepare your Raspberry Pi's operating system. If you bought your Pi as part of a kit then it may have come with NOOBS ("New Out Of Box Software") pre-installed on an SD memory card, in which case you can skip this step. If not, you'll either need to buy an SD memory card with the software pre-installed, or download the software to a memory card of your own, as outlined here.

1. To start with you will need a micro SD memory card with a capacity of at least 8GB. Using a desktop computer or laptop, download and install SD Formatter from www.sdcard.org and use it to format your memory card.

The easiest way to install the operating system on a new Raspberry Pi is to use NOOBS. You can download this at the Raspberry Pi Foundation's website.

2. Next, download NOOBS from www.raspberrypi.org (you'll find the software in the Downloads section of the website). It's useful to set your Desktop as the download destination, so you can find the file easily.

3. NOOBS will download as a Zip file, which you need to "extract" (open). Once you've extracted all the files, drag-and-drop them onto your SD card to copy them across.

< 33 >

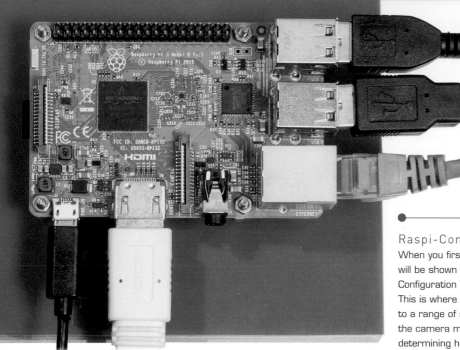

Raspi-Config

When you first boot into Raspbian you will be shown the Raspberry Pi Software Configuration Tool (or "raspi-config"). This is where you can make changes to a range of settings, such as enabling the camera module (when it's attached), determining how your Pi boots up, and other fundamental steps.

Making The Connections

With NOOBS installed on an SD card, you're ready to start playing with your Pi. You need to wire it all up first, though, so work your way through the following steps:

1. Plug your USB keyboard and mouse into two of your Raspberry Pi's USB sockets.

2. Attach your Raspberry Pi to your monitor using an HDMI cable or a VGA cable and an HDMI-to-VGA adaptor (for VGA monitors).

3. Insert your micro SD memory card into the slot on your Raspberry Pi, making sure it's the right way around.

4. Plug the power adaptor into the micro USB power connector. Your Raspberry Pi should spring to life immediately, as there is no on/off switch.

Installing Raspbian

Installing the Raspbian operating system is incredibly easy if you're using NOOBs. When your Raspberry Pi powers up for the first time you will be offered a choice of operating systems—simply choose *Raspbian*, followed by *Install*, and then click *OK* at the prompt box.

NOOBS will work its magic and install the Raspbian OS and other software for you. This will take about 10 to 15 minutes, but while you wait you can read the information being displayed in the setup window to get an insight into Raspbian.

< 34 >

Connecting To The Internet

You can connect your Raspberry Pi to the Internet using an Ethernet cable, in which case it will connect automatically to your network.

Alternatively, you can connect via Wi-Fi, either by using the built-in connectivity of a Raspberry Pi 3 (the easiest option); via a fully Pi-compatible dongle (the next best thing); or by attaching a Wi-Fi dongle that requires drivers to be installed (not generally recommended).

Assuming you're using a Raspberry Pi 3 (or a fully compatible dongle), connecting to Wi-Fi is as simple as left-clicking the network icon at the top right corner of the Raspbian desktop (on the menu bar) and choosing your network from the dropdown list. If no networks are found immediately, wait while your Pi scans for connection options; if it continues to struggle check that your router is on and within range.

If you're trying to connect to a secure network you'll be asked for a password or "key," which needs to be entered before you connect. After you've entered the key and pressed *OK* your Raspberry Pi will make the connection and you'll be online!

If you want to know the status of your Internet connection, why not build a Pi powered Internet Monitor, as seen on pages 144–147?

< 35 >

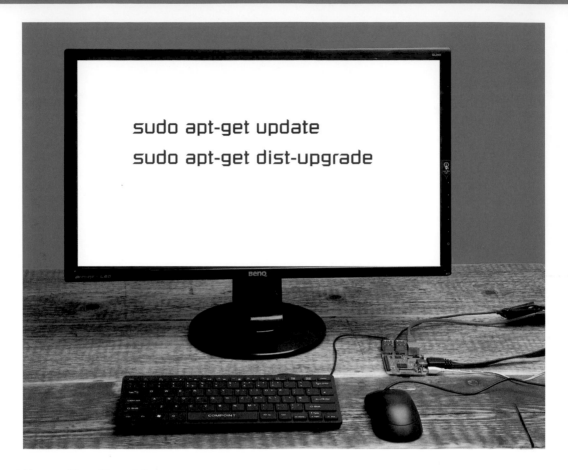

Upgrading Raspbian

If you want your Raspberry Pi to function at its best, you need to ensure it's running the latest operating system. The version that was installed during the previous steps might not necessarily be the most up-to-date version available, so it's worth running an upgrade routine.

Once you've connected your Pi to the Internet, check your Internet connection by opening the web browser. Having confirmed that you're connected to the Internet, open the terminal and type in the following command:

```
sudo apt-get update
```

Press the *Enter* key and your Raspberry Pi will start to download and install any updates. Once this is done, type in the following command:

```
sudo apt-get dist-upgrade
```

Press *Y* and *Enter* when asked and your Pi will get and install all the upgrades required.

The reason you need to upgrade your Raspbian is because newer versions will have had more bugs fixed and the overall performance will be enhanced, giving you the best experience. It is therefore a good idea to routinely run the upgrade and update processes.

< 36 >

Coding Basics

To be able to make the most of your Raspberry Pi, you will want to learn to code. Code is a set of instructions or rules for a computer to follow; in other words, it's a written language that the computer understands.

If you can write code—or "program"—then you can not only control a computer at every level, but you can also create your own software. So, if you learn to code with your Raspberry Pi you could make your own computer game, or write the rules that send commands to your own robot, or create your own music from scratch— the possibilities are (almost) endless!

Code is used to control and program your Raspberry Pi and other digital devices.

< 37 >

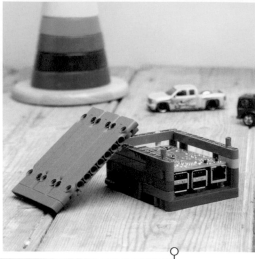

How To Code

To write code on a computer you will need to learn and use a programming language. A programming language is a version of computer code that both you and the computer can read.

There are numerous languages you can use to code a computer, and several of these work brilliantly with the Raspberry Pi. In fact, when you set up your new Raspberry Pi, languages such as C, C++, Java, and Ruby will be installed as standard, as well as Python, which is the officially recommended Raspberry Pi language for those learning to code for the first time. Scratch is also installed, and is even easier to get to grips with, making it especially good for younger coders.

Using Python

Python is a text-based programming language, which means you have to type in code using a special language. Fortunately, the Python language is as easy to learn as it is powerful.

When you start out using Python, you can use IDLE. This is a "Python development environment" that's installed with Raspbian on your Raspberry Pi. One of the great things

Although many Pi-based projects require some code, others do not, such as the Lunchbox Laptop (pages 172–175) and the LEGO® Technic Case (pages 212–215).

about IDLE is that it suggests corrections if your code isn't quite right.

To get started, call up the *Programming* menu from your Pi's desktop and select *Python 3* to open the latest version of Python.

Next, open *IDLE* and go to *File > New*. You should see what looks like a text window: this is where you can enter your Python code when you are first experimenting with the language.

But how do you learn to code? Well, lots of the projects in this book will help you learn by following examples and copying code, and there are plenty of books and websites that will help you with your coding as well. However, although it's quicker and easier to copy and paste code, if you type it out yourself you're likely to start understanding it quicker.

< 38 >

Command Lines

Your Raspberry Pi has a special tool called a command line interface, or "terminal" (the default application is LXTerminal). Although this looks like a regular text-editing window, it is really used to control your computer. In a way, a terminal provides an alternative means to interact with a computer to using a keyboard and mouse; instead of pointing and clicking to control your computer, you use text commands.

A terminal typically allows you to get deeper into the workings of your computer, making it a powerful and important way to take control of your Pi. Using a terminal will enable you to locate and run software, install new applications and libraries, get your built projects working in harmony, and much more besides. Many of the tutorials in this book will require you to enter commands: the terminal is the place to do it.

HOW THIS BOOK WORKS

At the end of this chapter—and in the chapters that follow—you will find a selection of exciting Raspberry Pi projects that will inspire you with your own builds. The projects range in complexity, from relatively straightforward, low-cost undertakings, through to advanced projects that demand more time, a greater financial investment, and a lot more skill to complete: these are the projects that will challenge even the most seasoned makers.

As well as inspirational builds from some of the best makers around, we have also included a selection of projects that are perfect for novices. With clearly written tutorials and easy-to-follow illustrations, these "Build It!" projects will walk you step-by-step through the process, helping you gain experience in making electronic circuits, entering command lines, and even writing code.

This may sound daunting if you've never programmed anything before, but to help you with the coding side of things there's a website dedicated to this book at:

quartoknows.com/page/raspberry-pi

Here you will find all the code you need for each of the "Build It!" projects, and—best of all—you can choose how you employ it.

If you're a coding novice, you can simply opt to "copy and paste" the code from the website, which will enable you to program your projects successfully, with just a couple of clicks of your mouse.

If you're feeling more adventurous, then you might want to input the code instead, keying in every line. Sure, it's going to take you longer to do it, and there's a greater risk of making mistakes, but by entering the code yourself—and going back to check and "debug" it—you will soon start to understand this new "language" you are speaking. And before you know it, you'll soon be creating code for your own bespoke projects and creations!

< 39 >

Build it!

Blinking LED

If you can make an LED blink, you will have demonstrated that you understand the fundamentals of electronics. It will also give you the opportunity to explore simple circuits and coding.

STATS

BUILDER	Inderpreet Singh
TIME TO BUILD	One hour
COST TO BUILD	Under $10 (plus Pi)
DIFFICULTY LEVEL	Beginner

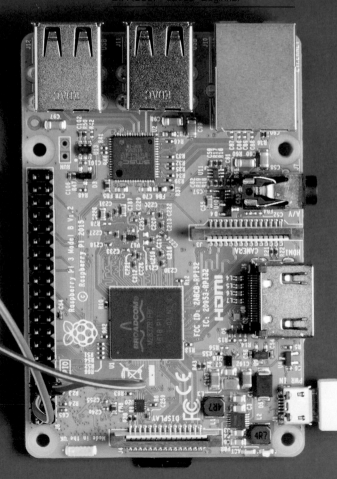

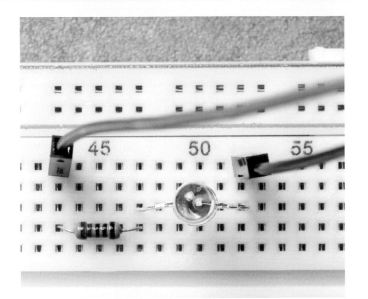

MATERIALS

→ Raspberry Pi (any model)

→ LED

→ 220 Ohm resistor

→ Breadboard

→ Two male-to-female jumper wires

The Project

If you've ever seen "Hello World" displayed on the screen of any kind of computer or gadget, you've spotted the technology world's longest running in-joke. Writing a "Hello World" program is something of a computing tradition: it can be used to prove that you understand the latest coding language; demonstrate that a newly designed computer system is working; or indicate some other "Eureka" moment.

In the world of electronics, the "Hello World" equivalent is to make an LED (light emitting diode) flash on and off. So what better way to get started with your Raspberry Pi than by assembling a simple electronics circuit board and writing a program that makes an LED flash?

The Builder

Inderpreet Singh has been tinkering with electronics for more than two decades, which has given him an in-depth experience of computers and electronic engineering. You can find another of his beginner projects—a Shutdown Button—on pages 44–47 (you can even reuse some of the parts from this project).

Get the code
quartoknows.com/pages/raspberry-pi

< 41 >

TUTORIAL

1. Set Up Your Pi

You'll need your Raspberry Pi ready
to go, with a keyboard and screen
attached and the Raspbian operating
system installed (see page 34). Keep
your Pi powered down for now.

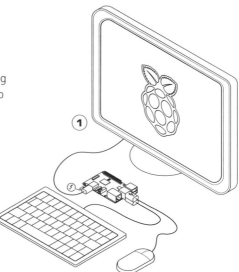

2. Make The Circuit

Take your breadboard, wires, LED, and
resistor, and connect them together as
shown. If you stick something in the wrong
hole, just pull it out again. That's the point
of electronics breadboards—they provide
you with a "reusable circuit board" that
allows you to experiment, learn, prototype,
and make mistakes!

3. Locate Your Pins

To get your LED flashing you will need to connect it—with
your resistor—between a GPIO pin and a "ground" pin.
Start by locating a ground pin (GND) and the GPIO 4 pin
(sometimes referred to as "Pin 7"). These pins are where
you will wire up your electronics circuit, as indicated
below: red is positive, and blue is the "ground."

1	+3V3	2	+5V
3	GPIO 2/SDA1	4	+5V
5	GPIO 3/SCL1	6	GND
7	GPIO 4	8	TXD0/GPIO 14
9	GND	10	RXD0/GPIO 15
11	GPIO 17	12	GPIO 18
13	GPIO 27	14	GND
15	GPIO 22	16	GPIO 23
17	+3V3	18	GPIO 24
19	GPIO 10/MOSI	20	GND
21	GPIO 9/MISO	22	GPIO 25
23	GPIO 11/SCLK	24	CE0#/GPIO 8
25	GND	26	CE1#/GPIO 7
27	GPIO 0/ID_SD	28	ID_SC/GPIO 1
29	GPIO 5	30	GND
31	GPIO 6	32	GPIO 12
33	GPIO 13	34	GND
35	GPIO 19/MISO	36	CE2#/GPIO 16
37	GPIO 26	38	MOSI/GPIO 20
39	GND	40	SCLK/GPIO 21

2 4 6 8 10 12 14 16 18 20 22 24 26 28 30 32 34 36 38 40

1 3 5 7 9 11 13 15 17 19 21 23 25 27 29 31 33 35 37 39

< 42 >

4. Add Your Code

Make sure you have the SD card containing the operating system slotted into your Pi and power it up. Once it has booted up, click on the computer monitor icon in the Application Launchbar at the top of the screen to open a terminal window.

Type the following command to open up a new Leafpad editor window, where you can enter your code:

```
leafpad blink.py
```

Then, use your Pi's web browser to navigate to the book's website and copy the project code. This code—which uses the Python programming language—will tell the LED to turn on and off.

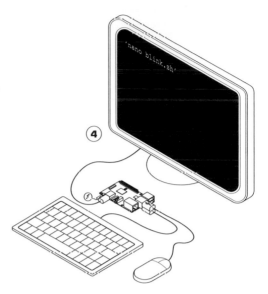

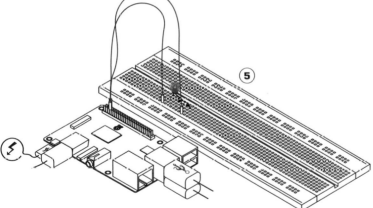

5. Testing

Once you have entered the code, exit the Leafpad editor and save when prompted. Go back to the terminal and type the following command:

```
sudo python3 blink.py
```

You will be prompted to enter a password: unless you have changed it, the default password is "raspberry." Once the password has been entered, the code will run and your LED will flash. Congratulations—you've just said "Hello World" using an LED and a Raspberry Pi!

TIPS

● Mastering a simple project like this will help you get to grips with a few basic skills before you move on to more intricate builds.

● Keep testing and checking your project as you go. If you test things at every stage, you're more likely to stay on track.

● There's nothing wrong with starting over if things don't work. Better still, if you do return to the start of your project (or an early stage of it) you'll be more likely to remember every lesson a project like this has to offer.

< 43 >

Build it!

Shutdown Button

Despite the Raspberry Pi's many strengths, it lacks something that is taken for granted on most other electronic devices: a power button.

STATS

BUILDER	Inderpreet Singh
TIME TO BUILD	1–2 hours
COST TO BUILD	Under $10 (plus Pi)
DIFFICULTY LEVEL	Beginner

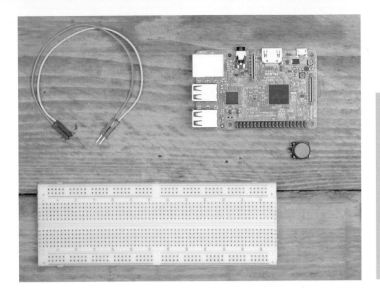

MATERIALS

→ Raspberry Pi (Pi 2 or Pi 3)
→ Breadboard
→ Momentary push button (the type that uses push for on and release for off)
→ Connecting wires

The Project

A power button has numerous benefits, which include protecting your projects from the damage that could be caused by the Pi suddenly powering down. This inspired Inderpreet to design a button that issues a "shutdown" command to the operating system, turning the Raspberry Pi off safely.

The Builder

Inderpreet Singh is an electronics engineer from Amritsar, India. He has been tinkering with electronics for more than 20 years and is devoted to sharing his projects and findings. His website, *Embedded Code*, is packed with insights for hobbyists, and is inspired by the idea that you don't need to spend a lot of money to do good work.

TIPS

● If in doubt, Google it! Thanks to the efforts of the Raspberry Pi community there is a lot of detailed information available.

● Prototype first, upgrade second. Use your breadboard and whatever components you have lying around to prototype your projects. When it works as you expect it to you can upgrade it— by buying better quality buttons or a case, for example.

● You can make this project using an early Pi 1, but you may need to choose different GPIO and ground pins as the earliest boards only had 26 pins.

Get the code
quadoknows.com/page/raspberry-pi

< 45 >

1. Mount The Button

Start by mounting the push button on the breadboard. If your push button has four terminals you'll need to use two that get connected when the button is pressed. Make the connections to the buttons using the connecting wires as shown.

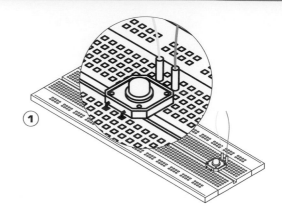

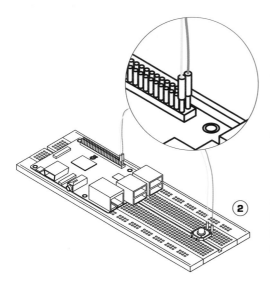

2. Select A GPIO Pin

Next, you'll need to select a GPIO. Here we are interested in using one of the pins to detect a button press: the button will be connected between the GPIO pin and the ground pin, so pressing the button reduces the voltage to zero.

For this project, select GPIO 21, which is at one end of the connector, right next to the ground pin (you are free to use any other unused GPIO). Use the connecting wires to complete the circuit, as shown here.

3. Code Your Pi

Boot up your Raspberry Pi and open a terminal window. Type the following command:

```
leafpad shutdown.py
```

This will open up a new Leafpad editor window. Type in the project code from this book's website, then save the file and close the terminal window.

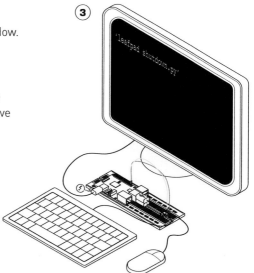

< 46 >

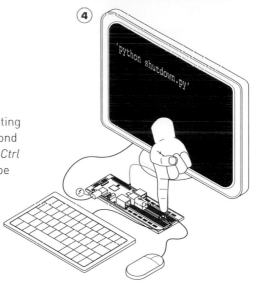

4. Test Your Script

Test your script by opening the terminal and typing:

`sudo python3 shutdown.py`

Press the shutdown button. A message saying "shutting down" should appear on screen and after a five-second delay your Raspberry Pi will shut down. If you press *Ctrl + C* before those five seconds are up, the script will be stopped, aborting the shutdown procedure.

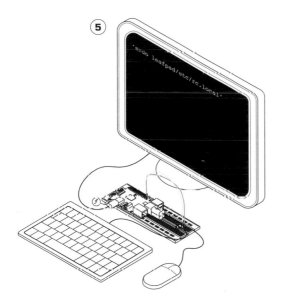

5. Activate On Startup

In order to make the shutdown button "active" when your Raspberry Pi starts up, you need to include it in an *rc.local* script. Open a new terminal and type the following command:

`sudo leafpad /etc/rc.local`

This will open the Leafpad editor, with the *rc.local* file loaded. At the end of the file (before *exit 0* in the code) add the following:

`sudo python3 /home/pi/shutdown.py &`

Save the file and exit Leafpad.

6. Success!

Reboot your Raspberry Pi and your shutdown button should be functioning. Congratulations! You've given your Raspberry Pi a simple, reliable, and extremely useful power button.

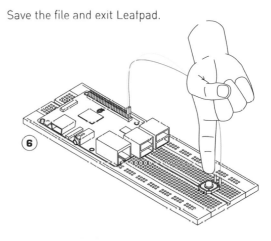

< 47 >

2

ROBOT PI
Raspbots and Piborgs to build

PiNoculars

What do you get if you combine a Raspberry Pi, a Pi camera module, an LCD touchscreen, and a pair of binoculars? "PiNoculars," of course!

STATS

BUILDER	Josh Williams
TIME TO BUILD	10 hours
COST TO BUILD	Approx. $100
DIFFICULTY LEVEL	Beginner

A Pi camera module sits over one of the binocular viewing lenses, enabling it to "see" through the binoculars. The Raspberry Pi can then record the image.

MATERIALS

→ Binoculars

→ Raspberry Pi

→ Raspberry Pi camera module

→ Raspberry Pi camera cable (medium length)

→ Adafruit 2.8" PiTFT capacitive touchscreen

→ Micro SD memory card (4GB+)

→ USB Wi Fi dongle

→ Ruler or calipers

→ ¼" thick Baltic birch (approx. 10" x 10" sheet)

→ 2 x small/medium rubber bands

→ Electrical tape

→ 3 x M2 x 25mm machine screws & nuts

→ 4 x M2 x 8mm machine screws & nuts

→ 4" of drinking straw

→ AA battery case (4 cells) with USB output

→ 4 x AA batteries

The Project

Josh's PiNoculars project originated when he was out with his wife driving in their car. Josh gets bored easily on long drives and motion sick if he reads, so is always looking for something to keep him occupied. On this occasion he had a Raspberry Pi with a camera module, binoculars, and duct tape with him, so simply combined the three and used the car to temporarily power his setup: "It was ugly, but it worked!"

From this humble prototype it was fairly simple to refine the build, which involved holding everything together using laser-cut Baltic birch and powering it with four AA cells.

It was also easy to find a convenient way of displaying images on the touchscreen and taking pictures, as Adafruit Industries and Phillip Burgess had written scripts and assembled a Raspberry Pi OS that do this perfectly.

How To Use This Idea

You don't need a laser cutter and precision-cut Baltic birch to make your own PiNoculars. Josh has also created instructions for a "quick and dirty" version using foam core and electrical tape: it isn't as rugged or as pretty, but it's just as effective.

< 51 >

The Builder

Josh Williams is a 35-year-old maker from Ann Arbor, MI. As a full-time facilitator at Makerspaces, his time is split between teaching and helping people to use tools safely, and developing workshops for kids. These workshops have so far included everything from forging bracelets to making felt plush monsters and origami-inspired robotic cranes.

Josh was initially given a Raspberry Pi as a gift by his father-in-law. The low cost has allowed him to experiment more freely than he might with a more expensive platform. To date he has produced a number of exciting projects, including SoilCam (which you can see on pages 110–113), and LEGO® Minecraft® EV3 Creeper Robot (his favorite project to date).

The electronics for the PiNoculars are mounted on laser-cut Baltic birch wood, but foamcore will also work.

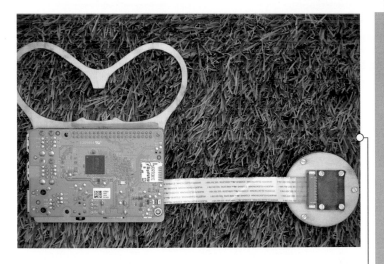

TIPS

- Calipers are amazing tools when you need to make accurate measurements. A ruler will do at a pinch, but when you're designing something small that has to fit another object, calipers will save you time.

- Make a prototype using basic materials. Having access to a laser cutter is great, but prototyping with card or foamcore is often quicker and can highlight problem areas before you spend time trying to make a "perfect" version.

- Measure everything twice. For this project it was important to work out the distance between the camera and Raspberry Pi before purchasing a camera cable—the stock version would have been too short.

It's worth checking the distance you need between the camera and Raspberry Pi. This setup required a medium length camera cable.

Josh's PiNoculars allow you to display images on the touchscreen and take pictures. This is perfect for nature walks!

< 53 >

RoboCroc

Built using an off-the-shelf kit and a child's
sandal, RoboCroc proves just how accessible
Raspberry Pi can be.

STATS

BUILDER	Mark Norwood
TIME TO BUILD	2 days
COST TO BUILD	Approx. $65
DIFFICULTY LEVEL	Beginner

The Project

Mark created RoboCroc using a CamJam Edukit 3. The kit provides the main components needed to create a robot, so all you have to add is a Raspberry Pi, a power supply, and a chassis (in this instance, a discarded child's sandal).

Mark plans to develop a mini *BattleBots* style unit of work for the students he teaches, where they will design, build, and program their own robots. The robots will each have balloons tied to their rear and will be armed with a pin with which to attack and pop their opponents' balloons. RoboCroc was a prototype for this bigger project.

Although CamJam provides all the Python code needed for its kit, Mark decided to translate it into Scratch, as that is a more accessible language for the students he works with. However, as a relatively inexperienced coder it still took some time for Mark to get it all to work using Scratch instead of Python.

MATERIALS

→ Raspberry Pi
→ CamJam Edukit 3
→ 2 x AA batteries to power the motors
→ Lightweight power pack to power the Raspberry Pi
→ Computer to access the Raspberry Pi via Wi-Fi
→ Robot chassis (in this instance an old sandal, a ruler, and some glue!)

This humble foam 'bot can be programmed to follow a line drawn on the floor; to move randomly, avoiding obstacles; or it can be controlled remotely by an operator.

//

The Code

RoboCroc utilizes Scratch code to make a GPIO pin "live," but Python can be used to achieve the same thing. Once you know how to "turn on" a GPIO pin using code, you can then use whatever other code you like in conjunction with this type of project.

//

< 55 >

RoboCroc's "brain" is a Wi-Fi enabled Raspberry Pi that sits inside the sandal.

A bigger challenge was working out a way to remotely access and control the on-board Raspberry Pi. As a robot can't have a monitor, keyboard, and mouse attached to it, Mark decided to use VNC software and Wi-Fi to access the Pi from a laptop. The problem here was that the Raspbian operating system had just been upgraded to Jessie. Although this was a great upgrade, it meant that none of the VNC instructions Mark found online would work. In the end he got a huge amount of help online.

The Builder

Mark Norwood is a teacher who lives in Leighton Buzzard in the English countryside. For the past 15 years he has been teaching young people who have been excluded from mainstream education.

During this time he has been asked to teach a wide variety of subjects, as well as introducing Computing as a subject at the small school he works in. For this, Mark set about creating an accessible curriculum that would stimulate and engage children with a wide range of severe behavioral difficulties.

< 56 >

Quite a bit of wiring is needed to get a robot like RoboCroc working, but there's plenty of support for the CamJam Edukit 3, so it's hard to go too far wrong.

The Raspberry Pi has since become an invaluable teaching tool for Mark, and his personal projects are always about experimenting to see whether he can transfer a concept to the classroom.

For Mark, the joy of Raspberry Pi projects comes from overcoming obstacles and bugs, getting a project to work, and then tweaking it to make it better. There is also an added satisfaction when the young people he teaches experience the same thrill of getting a project up and running.

How To Use This Idea

A robot simply needs two motors that you can turn on and off, which is usually achieved using a motor controller board attached to the GPIO pins. Once you can do this, a whole world of projects, devices, and inventions opens up to you. To get started, why not build the introductory Box Bot on pages 68–73?

< 57 >

CamTank

The CamTank is every young (and not-so-young) builder's dream: a smartphone-controlled, video-streaming tank that can drive and shoot BB pellets!

STATS

BUILDER	Chen Lu
TIME TO BUILD	200 hours
COST TO BUILD	Approx. $300
DIFFICULTY LEVEL	Intermediate

MATERIALS

CONTROL
- → Raspberry Pi Model B
- → Powered USB hub
- → USB webcam
- → Wi-Fi dongle
- → Female-to-male jumper cable

DRIVE
- → 2 x high torque continuous servos or motors (for two drive wheels)
- → ⅛" steel rod for wheel shafts
- → 10 x sleeve bearings
- → Springs (for suspension)

TURRET
- → Automatic BB gun
- → High torque mini DC motor
- → Micro servo for tilting up and down
- → ¼" steel rod (for gun barrel)

The Project

The CamTank is a project Chen had been hoping to build for years. It stemmed from his love of tanks: he has built a lot of scale models, but none of them was functional, and he didn't like any of the ready-made remote controlled tank toys on the market. He had tried modifying toy tanks in the past without any great success. This changed when Chen got his own 3D printer, as it enabled him to design and make his own parts.

The execution of the project was a challenge for Chen. Not only did it involve mechanical, electrical, and software engineering, but it was also his first Raspberry Pi project. As he isn't an expert in any of the necessary fields (and just a novice in some of them), he didn't know everything. For example, he didn't know the formulas for the gears and levers, so used simple trial and error instead. He also wasn't sure how code worked, so had to continually research and read about different

applications until he worked out what he needed. The key, he says, is to not be afraid of failure and to keep trying.

With so much effort required, it's unsurprising that Chen is very happy to have brought CamTank to fruition. He is

CamTank's turret can tilt up and down, giving it more flexibility when it comes to directing fire.

< 59 >

also grateful to the Raspberry Pi community, which helped him to learn what he needed and fix any problems he encountered—thanks to the community he wasn't starting entirely from scratch.

After Chen published his project online, it featured on a number of maker websites, which not only validated the project, but also showed doubting friends that he wasn't wasting his time and money.

His passion for making was strengthened further when he took the CamTank to local maker fairs and got to see how excited kids were when they saw it in action.

Since he completed his CamTank, Chen has also used Raspberry Pi to make a media center, a NAS server, and create some home automation. An upgraded version of the tank is also being planned!

A webcam is used on top for video streaming through a smartphone app.

< 60 >

Springs are used to push the axle and create a simple suspension mechanism. This helps the tank's tracks make it over obstacles.

Chen would like to add some tread to the next version of his tank's 3D-printed caterpillar tracks, for better traction.

< 61 >

CamTank's weapons system consists of a stripped down automatic airsoft gun with a steel rod for a barrel.

The Builder

Chen Lu is from Jinan, China, but works as a UX (user experience) designer in Louisville, KY. As a child, he was always curious about how things worked and would tear apart almost any electronic item he could, analyzing it and then putting it back together.

While working toward a degree in Electrical Engineering, Chen realized that what really appealed to him was the creative side of electronics. He subsequently went on to study for a master's degree in Industrial Design at SCAD (Savannah College of Art and Design), which gave him knowledge in both design and engineering that he could apply to his projects.

How To Use This Idea

Because you drive CamTank in a first-person view using a smartphone, it has plenty of practical applications, such as exploring otherwise inaccessible spaces or home security. It also has several more frivolous options, such as playing with your cat or dog, or having fun with friends.

You could always buy a toy tank, but making your own Pi-based version is much more fun!

< 62 >

Raspberry Pi HAL 9000

A Raspberry Pi, some off-the-shelf components, and a stylish acrylic case combine to recreate the infamous sentient computer from *2001: A Space Odyssey*.

STATS

BUILDER	Djordje Ungar
TIME TO BUILD	Months of organizing, followed by a two-day build
COST TO BUILD	Approx. $100
DIFFICULTY LEVEL	Intermediate

Keeping the insides of a project like this tidy and well secured will ensure the build lasts—and works—for as long as possible.

MATERIALS

→ Raspberry Pi 2 Model B

→ Raspberry Pi power cord

→ Wi-Fi USB dongle (with antenna)

→ Wireless mini-speaker

→ USB digital 6 LED webcam

→ ⅛" thick black acrylic sheet (approx. 16" x 8")

→ USB external sound card

→ Wide-angle lens adaptor

→ Metallic spray paint

The Project

Like its namesake, Djordje Ungar's Raspberry Pi HAL 9000 is a "Heuristically programmed ALgorithmic computer." This is a humorous definition of what is in essence a digital assistant powered by Jasper, the open-source platform that can be used to create always-on, voice-controlled applications.

As the name suggests, Djordje's creation assumes the form of HAL 9000, the iconic, maniacal, and curiously lovable computer from Stanley Kubrick's classic sci-fi movie, *2001: A Space Odyssey*. The Raspberry Pi HAL 9000 can deliver many of the classic lines that made his celluloid counterpart so infamous!

Raspberry Pi HAL 9000 is equipped with Wi-Fi, a webcam, a microphone, and a Bluetooth audio speaker. Users can give it voice commands, such as asking it to check the weather, see if any new emails are waiting, play a .WAV file, take a webcam snapshot and mail it their way, and many more things besides.

//

The Code

A handful of scripts and software is needed to transform Raspberry Pi HAL 9000 from a pretty model to a working megalomaniac computer. Djordje has a script you can download for recording .WAV files from the microphone and another for saving webcam screenshots. You'll also need to install Jasper (jasperproject.github.io).

//

< 65 >

The first time Djordje heard synthesized speech, he immediately thought of granting a home computer the voice of HAL 9000. This was long before the Raspberry Pi had gone public, so the idea lay dormant, but Djordje couldn't quite shake the notion of crafting his own power-crazed computer.

Once Raspberry Pi arrived, and mainstream digital assistants such as Siri, Alexa, and OK Google started to appear, the basic idea of Raspberry Pi HAL 9000 gained traction in this ambitious maker's mind. When Djordje found Jasper, he realized it was time to harness the potential of Raspberry Pi to craft his own HAL 9000.

The Raspberry Pi HAL 9000 was Djordje's first substantial project using the pocket-sized Pi, so rather than rushing straight in, he spent a good deal of time familiarizing himself with the technology.

Djordje also did a lot of research into HAL's distinctive look, examining dozens of movie stills from Kubrick's film. Originally, Djordje considered building an exact replica of HAL 9000, but he quickly realized that without seeing the original movie prop he would never achieve the level of authenticity he wanted. Instead, he decided to go with a build that would approximate the real HAL's form.

Although this project is technologically impressive, what makes it stand out is the polished production standard of its casing.

The Builder

Although he is a programmer by day, by night Djordje Ungar describes himself as a "digital alchemist." It's an appropriate way to sum up everything that interests him, as he spends his time as a hobby artist, animator, musician, game developer, hacker, and all-round tinkerer.

Djordje also runs what he calls a "digital laboratory" for coding experiments, and creates a diverse array of artworks that often have technological or playful themes.

Djordje is not limited by those definitions, though: he is a devotee to all things creative and the process of bringing ideas to life, such as game characters, robots, and software programs.

When designing a project that sits inside a case, remember that you'll need extra space around the Raspberry Pi for any cables and dongles that may protrude from it.

How To Use This Idea

A great deal of the charm of the Raspberry Pi HAL 9000 is its gorgeous housing, which replicates the style of the film that inspires it. But the case also adds a great deal of effort and a little extra to the budget. If you want to reproduce the functions without spending as much time or money, you could use a pre-existing case, card box, or even a food storage tub instead.

TIPS

● Use sticky tape on the outer seams of the case to hold it together while you fix it permanently from the inside using high-strength glue. The sticky tape will prevent the glue from leaking onto the outside of the case, which will give you perfect seams.

● If any glue does leak out and stain the acrylic case, use an acrylic polishing paste or any abrasive equivalent to remove it. Djordje used toothpaste, cotton pads, and a lot of rubbing to remove some marks from his case!

< 67 >

 **Build it!**

Box Bot

Would you like to make your own simple robot?
Then look no further than Box Bot, which is a great
introduction to the world of Pi-based robotics.

STATS

BUILDER	Will Freeman
TIME TO BUILD	2–4 hours
COST TO BUILD	Approx. $65 (including Pi)
DIFFICULTY LEVEL	Beginner–Intermediate

MATERIALS

→ Two wired DC motors

→ Two wheels compatible with motors

→ CamJam Motor Controller Board

→ Ball caster with coupling

→ 4 x AA battery box

→ Tough card box with lid

→ Double-sided foam tape

→ Raspberry Pi

The Project

Just like RoboCroc (see pages 54–57), Box Bot has a CamJam EduKit 3 at its core. We're only using some of the components for this "get you started" build, but by adding the rest of the kit's contents the 'bot can also follow a line across the floor, sense distance to avoid collisions, and—with a little extra hacking—even be operated wirelessly using a video game controller. You may even want to add extra features that aren't part of the original kit.

The Builder

Will Freeman doesn't pretend to be an expert in robotics, but he put this lo-fi robot together in a single afternoon, proving just how easily the Raspberry Pi puts impressive technology within your reach.

TIPS

● Marking "front," "back," "left," and "right" inside your box will make it easy for you to tell which way around things should be when you move them around.

● If you put some weight over your robot's wheels it will improve their traction: positioning your battery box and other internal parts above the wheels will help.

● Use a box with a strong, hinged lid so you can continue to access the parts as you build, without your box falling apart.

Get the code
quartoknows.com/page/raspberry-pi

< 69 >

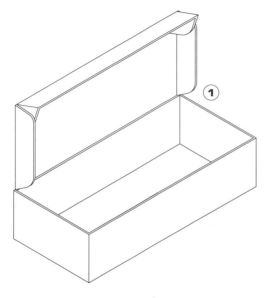

1. Choose Your Chassis
A card box makes a great body for your robot, but you need one with enough space to fit the Raspberry Pi, battery box, and wiring. If you don't want your robot to be tethered, you'll also need room for additional parts.

2. Add Motors & Wheels
Attach your motors, wheels, and the ball castor roller to the underside of the box, securing them with double-sided foam tape. The wheels sit at the front, and the castor wheel at its rear. Cut two small holes on the underside of the box so you can thread the motor's cables through, as shown in the illustration.

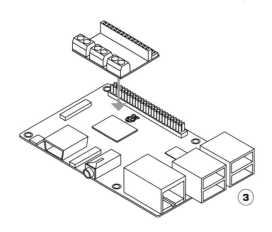

3. Connect The Controller Board
The Motor Controller Board connects to the GPIO pins of your Raspberry Pi 3 as shown. If you have a different Pi model, with an alternative number of pins, visit the Cambridge Raspberry Jam website for connection details.

< 70 >

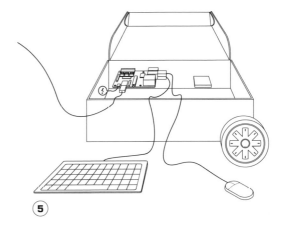

(5)

4. Wire It Up

Make sure you have the batteries inserted, but the battery box is turned off. The wires of the battery box must be attached as shown. Connect your right motor to "Motor A" on the Motor Controller Board and the left motor to "Motor B." For now, it doesn't matter which way around the motor's wires go.

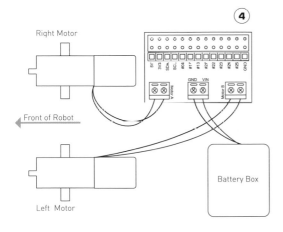

(4)

Right Motor

Front of Robot

Left Motor

Battery Box

5. Code The Wheels

The Raspberry Pi's GPIO pins operate the motors. We're using GPIOs 9 and 10 to control Motor A (right side motor) and GPIOs 7 and 8 to control Motor B (left side motor). Hook your Raspberry Pi up to a power supply, screen, mouse, and keyboard, and enter the following commands into a terminal window to make a directory for all your code for the robot:

```
cd ~
mkdir EduKitRobotics
cd EduKitRobotics
```

Then, type the following to create a new Python script in the Nano editor:

```
nano 3-motors.py
```

Now, go to this book's website and enter the *Box Bot 1* code for this project. When you've entered the code press *Ctrl + X* then *Y*, followed by *Enter* to save the file.

< 71 >

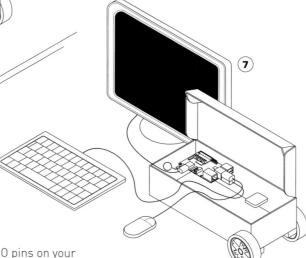

6. Test The Wheels

With your fledgling robot still connected to the mouse, keyboard, and screen, turn on the battery box. Support your 'bot so its wheels are off the ground and enter the following in a terminal window to run your Python script:

```
sudo python3 3-motors.py
```

Both wheels should run forward one second. If either wheel is turning the wrong way, simply swap the two wires connecting the problem wheel's motor to the Motor Controller Board. Once both wheels are running correctly you've got a robot that can drive forward in a straight line!

7. Add Direction

Each of your motors uses two GPIO pins on your Raspberry Pi. Turning those pins on and off in different combinations will enable your robot to move forward, backward, left, and right. Get ready to create a new Python script in Nano by entering the following into a terminal window:

```
cd ~/EduKitRobotics
nano 4-driving.py
```

Head back to this book's website, and enter the *Box Bot 2* code. Again, when you are done, press *Ctrl + X* then *Y*, followed by *Enter* to save the file.

Enter the following in a terminal to run the code (your robot won't move, but it will check the code for errors):

```
sudo python3 4-driving.py
```

< 72 >

8. Add Movement

To move your robot, you need to edit the code you entered in the previous step. Add the following lines, just before the last line of the code, which reads **GPIO.cleanup()**:

```
Forwards()
time.sleep(1)
Backwards()
time.sleep(1)
StopMotors()
```

Now, run the script again using **python3 4-driving.py**. Your robot will move forward for one second and then backward for one second. Make sure your Raspberry Pi's power supply cable is long enough to allow your robot freedom of movement.

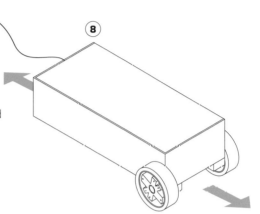

9. Take Control

You'll need to adapt the code again to add left and right control. Edit your **driving.py** code one last time, so it matches the *Box Bot 3* code on this book's website: you'll notice some new lines that add left and right movement.

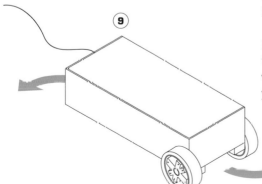

Run the code again (using **Python3 4-driving.py**) and your robot should take a snaking journey across the floor.

Now, try editing the numbers entered alongside **time.sleep** in the last section of the code. These numbers determine how long—in seconds—your robot moves in different ways.

By changing this code you can plot a route for your robot, before heading to the CamJam website (camjam.me) to learn how to take your project to the next level.

< 73 >

3
GAME PI
Make your own games consoles

PIK3A Retro Gaming Table

Spanner Spencer's weekend project transformed a low-cost table into a high-end arcade experience.

STATS

BUILDER	Spanner Spencer
TIME TO BUILD	One weekend
COST TO BUILD	Approx. $120
DIFFICULTY LEVEL	Beginner–Intermediate

When you're deciding where to position your screen, stick, and buttons, the most important consideration is what's comfortable for you during long gameplay sessions.

MATERIALS

→ Raspberry Pi 3

→ Micro SD card

→ IKEA Lack table

→ 17" 4:3 LCD monitor

→ Ball top arcade joystick

→ Arcade buttons
   (4 game buttons,
   1 coin button)

→ "1 player" button

→ USB encoder for joystick
   & buttons

→ Speakers

→ Volume control

→ IEC mains cable

→ IEC panel mount power inlet

→ 5V PSU

→ Micro USB cable

→ 21" x 21" clear acrylic sheet

The Project

"Cocktail tables" that combine a piece of functional furniture with an arcade game were seen regularly in cafés and bars when arcades were the face of the video games industry. It was this iconic form of gaming hardware that Spanner Spencer set out to recreate with his PIK3A Retro Gaming Table.

The software side of the project was already covered by *RetroPie*, which allows users to play retro games on their Raspberry Pi by installing various emulators and ROMs. However, Spanner still needed something suitable to recreate the classic arcade experience.

//

The Code
There's no code for this project: at the heart of the PIK3A table is the RetroPie Raspberry Pi gaming software, which you can download for free from retropie.org.uk.

//

< 77 >

Any arcade stick mechanism
designed to be installed
in a full-sized arcade
cabinet should work for
this project.

The answer came in the form
of a "Lack" table from Swedish
furniture store IKEA. Spanner
cut holes in his new table
for an LCD monitor, arcade
joystick, and buttons, and then
tucked his Raspberry Pi 3
inside. He covered the Lack's
surface with a clear acrylic
sheet to keep everything
tidy, and this also lets the
PIK3A serve one of its most
important functions: as a
cocktail table that people

can put their drinks on, right
over the screen.

As the PIK3A is a project that
can be thrown together in a
single weekend (IKEA queues
permitting!), it's proved wildly
popular. Countless people have
built their own, and Spanner
currently has a second version
under way that will support
two-player gaming and output
to a TV when needed.

< 78 >

With a clear acrylic sheet over the screen, Spanner's PIK3A Gaming Table remains usable as a table, so is not just a games machine.

Color-coding your buttons is a great way to remember which is which. Here, for example, the yellow buttons could be "A" and "B," the most common buttons used by arcade games.

TIPS

● Think before you build! Turn the monitor brightness and contrast to full before inserting it into the table, as you won't be able to reach the controls easily (if at all) once it is in position.

● Choose your buttons carefully. The Lack coffee table is only 50mm deep, and traditional arcade buttons—which commonly have a microswitch clipped to the bottom of a lengthy actuator—would stick out of the bottom of the table. Instead, try and track down buttons that have a built-in microswitch.

< 79 >

The Builder

As a result of his work as a games journalist, Spanner Spencer emerged as a respected name in the technology industries. Today, the former electronics engineer is a writer and community manager at *element14*, a thriving online hub for electronics collaborations.

It's hardly surprising that Spanner was immediately drawn to the Raspberry Pi when it was first released. The collective of designers, coders, and creative people that gathered around the Pi proved irresistible to a community manager, especially as *element14* is owned by Premier Farnell, the company that makes and supplies the Raspberry Pi!

How To Use This Idea

If you don't have the money—or space—for a gaming table, you can install a screen, stick, buttons, and Pi in almost anything that has enough internal capacity. You can also forgo a built-in screen and make a simple, console-sized games player that you can plug into a monitor using HDMI.

Spanner's table only offers one-player gaming, but he's already got a two-player option under development.

< 80 >

!

WARNING

A ROM can be described broadly as a game file. However, while you can find ROMs for classic retro games online, it is illegal to download them unless they have been officially released into the public domain. Nintendo has a lengthy legal document covering its intellectual property, which clearly states it has not released its games in this way!

< 81 >

Micro Arcade Cabinet

This diminutive arcade cabinet will fit on your desktop and is stuffed with classic games—and a Raspberry Pi!

STATS

BUILDER	Marco Tan
TIME TO BUILD	200 hours (including all design and prototyping)
COST TO BUILD	Approx. $200
DIFFICULTY LEVEL	Intermediate–Advanced

< 82 >

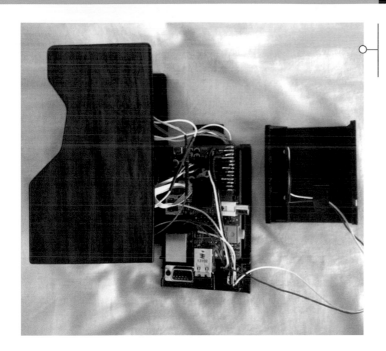

With such a compact build, the cabinet had to be designed carefully so there was room for the Raspberry Pi and other components.

The Project

When Marco wanted to build himself an arcade cabinet it was important that it fitted on his desk, so he could take a quick break from work to play a retro game from the golden era of the arcades. To achieve this he combined a Raspberry Pi with a custom, 3D-printed "micro" arcade cabinet that could sit in the palm of one hand. The result is not only beautiful to look at, but is also fully functional, with a clear screen, working controls, a built-in speaker, and even tiny lights that bathe it in the warm glow that once filled arcades across the world.

Putting the diminutive pieces together was fairly complicated, but the effort was well worth it. Despite its understated size, Marco's creation works very well for full-sized human hands, but there is one lingering problem—if you have one sitting on your desk, you won't get much work done!

MATERIALS
➔ Raspberry Pi
➔ Cabinet & buttons
➔ 2.5" TFT screen
➔ Mini joystick
➔ Inkjet decal paper

//

The Code

You'll barely need to enter a line of code for this project, but you will need to learn about game emulation. A great place to start is with the Retro Games Station project that appears on pages 96–99.

//

< 83 >

The Builder

Tinkering started at a very young age for Marco. He could rarely resist taking his toys apart to see what made them work, and before long he was fascinated by electronics and mechanics. It's a habit that's stayed with the Los Angeles-based designer and maker for a lifetime, during which he's worked on a range of projects, including remote-controlled contraptions, a Geiger counter, beautiful Nixie displays, and all manner of clocks.

However, despite the level of detail in his projects, Marco isn't a professional engineer or programmer. In fact, the Micro Arcade Cabinet is his first Raspberry Pi creation, which proves that you don't need to be an expert or have a long history with the Pi to achieve wonderful things!

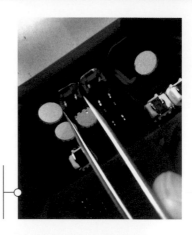

Working at a diminutive scale creates all kinds of challenges, such as the need for tweezers to fit some of the components.

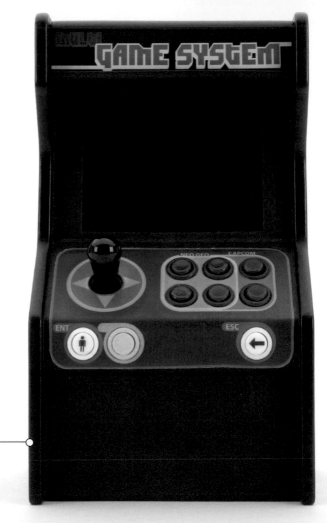

Putting some of the less frequently used buttons (such as "start" and "go back") on the front of the cabinet will leave space by the joystick for your fingers to hit the all-important gameplay buttons.

< 84 >

With a bit of experimentation
(and some tiny speakers!)
even a small build can
contain plenty of hardware.

TIPS

- Test all your software and hardware for functionality before assembly. This will save you having to take everything apart if you find a problem.

- 3D-printed parts emerge from the printer with a rough finish, so you will need to sand them down. For a perfectly smooth surface, try combining wet sanding and paint layering.

- When you're working with small parts it's important to work on a clean, tidy work surface, above a neat, hard floor. That will make it easier to locate any components that you drop.

How To Use This Idea

Ironically, keeping this tiny arcade cabinet so small also makes it quite intricate and expensive. If you scale things up, you will find parts are more widely available and this can decrease the overall cost.

< 85 >

$20 Portable Games Console

Thanks to the Raspberry Pi Zero, you can build a working handheld games console for less than the price of one big-budget game!

STATS

BUILDER	Tyler Spadganske
TIME TO BUILD	15–20 hours
COST TO BUILD	Approx. $20 (including Pi Zero)
DIFFICULTY LEVEL	Intermediate–Advanced

Tyler's $20 Portable Games
Console runs RetroPie, which
enables you to play classic
games from a variety of retro
console systems.

The Project

Numerous gaming-orientated projects have been made using a Raspberry Pi, but you'd be hard pressed to find one as affordable as Tyler Spadgenske's $20 Portable Games Console. Tyler set himself the challenge of building a handheld console that could run all of his favorite classic games, yet would cost him just $20 or less.

Like many Raspberry Pi gaming projects, the start point for this portable games machine is RetroPie, which Tyler installed on a Raspberry Pi Zero—the smallest and least expensive version of a Pi. To save money, very common or cheap parts were used, such as the battery, charging circuit, and even the small LCD screen. Custom circuitry also helped minimize the cost,

MATERIALS

→ Raspberry Pi Zero
→ 2.4" 240 x 320 pixel TFT display
→ Lithium-ion battery
→ Prototyping breadboard
→ 2¾" x 3½" perfboard
→ Charging circuit
→ Micro USB breakout
→ 3V–5V DC-DC step-up boost converter
→ 8 single pole, single throw (SPST) pushbuttons

///

The Code

Tyler's $20 Portable Games Console uses the same RetroPie software as most of the projects in this chapter. There's no code needed, just the software to install and a few simple commands to enter.

///

< 87 >

Four simple white buttons
at the right side of the
case emulate the classic
button configuration found
on Nintendo's popular SNES
console from the early 1990s.

How To Use This Idea
Instead of using a homemade
case, you could repurpose an
old handheld device. Fitting a
Raspberry Pi inside a Nintendo
Gameboy case is a popular (and
challenging) gaming project.

and Tyler housed everything
in a 3D-printed case that
he printed himself, paying
homage to the controller from
the original Super Nintendo
Entertainment System (SNES).

Of course, cutting costs may
not necessarily produce the
most refined result, but you
could easily improve the
quality of your handheld
console by spending a little
more. An additional investment
could get you a smarter
case, for example, or better
components, or make the
entire construction process

a little simpler by using
ready-made circuits. For Tyler,
though, this low-cost device
does everything that he set out
to achieve: it allows him to play
his favorite games and it came
in at less than $20, including
the cost of a Pi!

The Builder
Tyler Spadgenske is emerging
as one of the most talented
Raspberry Pi project builders
out there: as well as this build
he is also the talent behind the
popular Tytelli Smartphone
that you can see on pages
162–165.

< 88 >

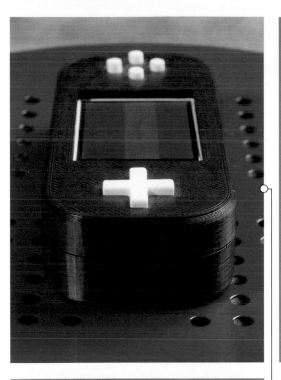

TIPS

- Setting yourself a limit for a project—such as a budget or timescale—can improve your creation, as it can help you focus more on what you need to get done and/or how much you can spend.

- Don't have a 3D printer? Many online services now print to order, so getting a custom enclosure might be easier than you think. However, this will easily put you over the $20 budget.

- As an alternative to a 3D-printed case you could try using acrylic, wood, or even card to make your own.

However, he is always open to learning from other builders and Raspberry Pi experts, and this project took inspiration from both the PiGrrl from Adafruit, and Ben Heck's renowned Raspberry Pi Portable. What makes Tyler's creation stand out from the crowd, though, is its ultra-low cost—$20 is around one fifth of the normal budget for a Raspberry Pi-based portable gaming device.

To keep his costs to a minimum, Tyler printed the black case and contrasting white controls himself.

< 89 >

Meccano Rubik's Shrine

Wilbert and Maxim's Meccano Rubik's
Shrine can solve a Rubik's cube in just
ten seconds—and it looks great while
it's doing it!

STATS

BUILDER	Wilbert Swinkels & Maxim Tsoy
TIME TO BUILD	5 months
COST TO BUILD	Approx. $950
DIFFICULTY LEVEL	Advanced

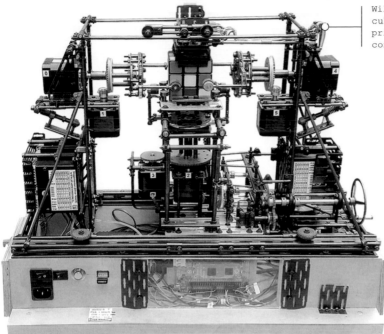

Wilbert's first Rubik's cube solver was made primarily out of FAC-System construction set parts.

The Project

Wilbert Swinkels and Maxim Tsoy's "Rubik's Shrine" is a Rubik's cube solving machine made primarily from Meccano. Thanks to the Raspberry Pi it can operate as a standalone device, and is capable of handling any scrambled cube. It achieves this incredible feat using a Raspberry Pi with a camera module, which together detect and recognize the colors of the faces of the cube. Using this information, the solving algorithm provides a solution in the form of a string of cube rotations. Mechanical grippers that are capable of gripping and rotating the cube execute these rotations, "solving" the cube.

//

The Code

For the Rubik's Shrine, Wilbert and Maxim created a Python/C version of Horbert Kociemba's "Two-Phase Algorithm" (aka the *Kociemba Algorithm*). If you intend to make your own cube, both the original and adapted algorithms are available online via meccanokinematics.net.

//

MATERIALS

- → Meccano (various)
- → 6 x NEMA14 hybrid stepper motors
- → 1 x NEMA17 hybrid stepper motor
- → 7 x DRV 8825 stepper drivers
- → Meanwell 220–240V AC to 24V DC power supply
- → Raspberry Pi
- → Raspberry Pi camera
- → Raspberry Pi 7" touchscreen
- → Teensy 3.2 USB development board
- → 2 x 12V LEDs to illuminate the cube during color detection
- → Various switches, start button & wiring

< 91 >

The Meccano Rubik's Shrine grew out of an earlier build, with the later incarnation featuring much faster color recognition. In spite of the considerable weight of the parts, acceleration, and deceleration become quite challenging: they can solve a cube in ten seconds, which is—as far as Wilbert and Maxim are aware—the fastest three-gripper solver in existence.

Shortly before they began their project the Raspberry Pi Foundation had announced its 7-inch touchscreen. This fitted perfectly with the builders' plans and the two-man team was pleasantly surprised to find that the screen worked without any problems. After a couple of nights they had a nice-looking touch user interface written in Kivy code, which also features a number of cube patterns, so in addition to solving the cube the machine can be asked to show a cube with a pattern instead.

Aligning the three grippers relative to each other is crucial for the device to work, especially given the high speed they move at.

Color detection was one of the most challenging parts of the project. Eventually, homemade sensors were used, as off the shelf analog ones were not up to the job.

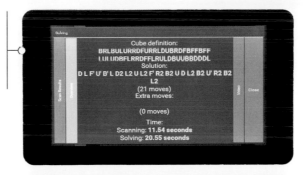

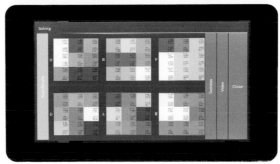

After making their first cube solver, Wilbert and Maxim uploaded a video of it to YouTube and within a month it had been viewed more than 100,000 times. The pair was massively encouraged by the reaction to this early iteration, especially by people who could hardly believe a machine could solve a Rubik's cube.

The current Meccano Rubik's Shrine was first exhibited at 2016's International Meccano Exhibition in Skegness, UK.

The Builder

Wilbert Swinkels is an architect from the Netherlands. As a youngster he was always interested in creative building using Meccano and LEGO®, and as a teenager was a proficient model maker.

In his professional career he became intrigued by modular building systems and this fascination led him back to Meccano, as well as to the more sophisticated

FAC-system construction sets. These systems offered Wilbert the tools he needed to prototype and design kinematical art, and study the architecture of machines.

Wilbert learned about Raspberry Pi through his friend and gifted programmer, Maxim Tsoy. As Wilbert has limited programming skills, Maxim worked as the Rubik's Shrine's programmer, developing and modifying the code needed to run the project.

How To Use This Idea

Making Raspberry Pi projects using modular systems is a great idea, and LEGO® is a good all-round material. In fact, LEGO could be used to create a less expensive Rubik's solver, because it's the coding that does a lot of the "heavy lifting" here.

< 93 >

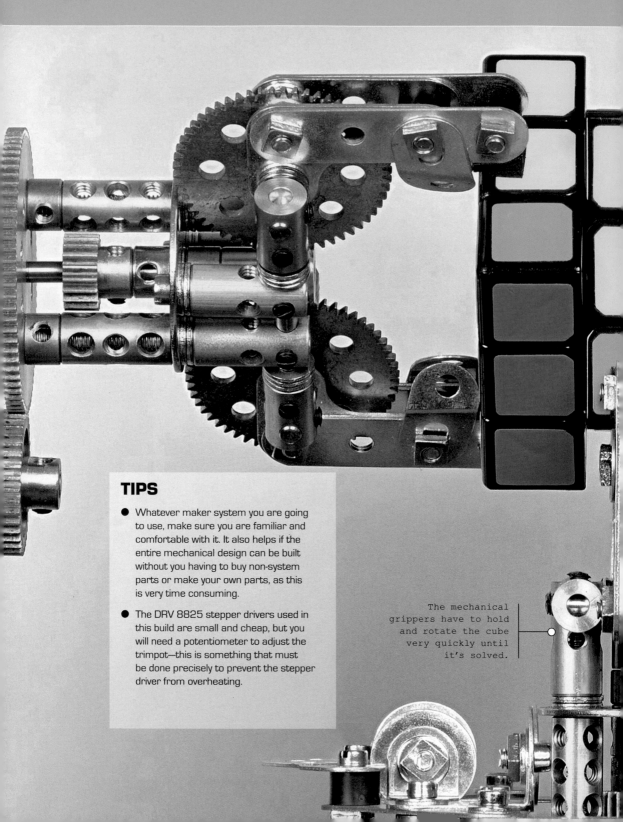

TIPS

● Whatever maker system you are going to use, make sure you are familiar and comfortable with it. It also helps if the entire mechanical design can be built without you having to buy non-system parts or make your own parts, as this is very time consuming.

● The DRV 8825 stepper drivers used in this build are small and cheap, but you will need a potentiometer to adjust the trimpot—this is something that must be done precisely to prevent the stepper driver from overheating.

The mechanical grippers have to hold and rotate the cube very quickly until it's solved.

				grab				Rotate CW	Open
								Rotate CCW	Close
				release				R is opened vertical	
								Rotate CW	Open
Menu	Solve	Archive	Debug	scan				Rotate CCW	Close
								D is opened horizontal	
				spin				Rotate CW	Open
								Rotate CCW	Close
								Table is raised	
				shoot				Raise	Lower

Maxim's programming
abilities perfectly
complement Wilbert's
mechanical skills to make
the project so spectacular.

Build it!

Retro Games Station

Your Raspberry Pi isn't just a tiny computer: with a few simple steps it can play an entire collection of retro games from a wide range of consoles.

STATS

BUILDER	Will Freeman
TIME TO BUILD	1–2 hours
COST TO BUILD	$70 (including Pi)
DIFFICULTY LEVEL	Beginner

MATERIALS

→ Raspberry Pi
→ USB memory stick
→ USB keyboard and mouse
→ USB gamepad (or controller of your choice)
→ Ethernet cable/Wi-Fi dongle
→ 8GB micro SD card
→ Case for your Pi (optional)
→ HDMI cable

The Project

There are countless classic video games that have stood the test of time, but how can you access these icons of video gaming history? Well, you could invest in several old consoles, track down some dusty cartridges, and start playing on the original hardware. Or you could turn your Raspberry Pi into a Retro Games Station.

To achieve this you need to use what is known as an "emulator," which essentially makes your Pi think it is a different computer. For example, a Super Nintendo emulator would cause your Pi to behave like a Super Nintendo, enabling you to run downloaded Super Nintendo games, or "ROMS" (although you must make sure it is lawful to use those ROMs!).

The Retro Games Station can go one better than that, though: it can make your Raspberry Pi behave like a whole *range* of classic games consoles, rather than one specific machine.

The Builder

Will Freeman is a video games journalist and keen collector of retro video games. Arcade games are his self-confessed obsession, and he can often be found toiling to climb the leaderboard of a vintage shoot 'em up. Will is also one of the authors of this book, and a fan of the Raspberry Pi since the earliest public prototypes.

WARNING

Although you can find ROMs for a whole range of classic games online, not all of them have been officially released into the public domain, in which case it is illegal to download them.

Get the code
quartoknows.com/page/raspberry-pi

< 97 >

TUTORIAL

1. Download RetroPie

For this build we're using a free piece of software called RetroPie. Using a laptop or desktop computer, head over to retropie.org.uk/download and choose the version of RetroPie you need, based on your Raspberry Pi model. You will actually be downloading an "SD image," which is a complete system built on top of the Raspberry Pi's Raspbian OS.

Once it's downloaded, the file will need "extracting," which means converting the .gz file into an .img (image) file that you can use. You can do the extraction using a program such as 7-Zip (from www.7-zip.org).

2. Put RetroPie On An SD Card

The next step is to install the image file onto a micro SD card. Start by inserting the SD card into your computer's card reader (using a card adaptor if necessary) and format it using SD Formatter, which you can download at www.sdcard.org.

Once your card is formatted, use Etcher to copy the RetroPie image to your micro SD card. Etcher is a free piece of software that is available for Windows, MacOS, and Linux. It can be downloaded from etcher.io.

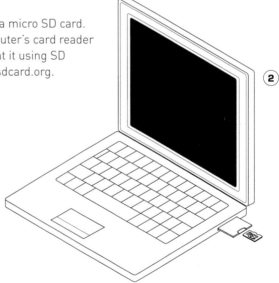

TIPS

- Be sure to visit the official RetroPie website for more information on emulation, ROMs, and using the platform.

- Keep an eye on the blinking indicator light on your USB stick; this will stop you pulling it out before your games are ready.

- You can build this idea into your own casing to make a homebrew gaming machine similar to the $20 Portable Games Console, Micro Arcade Cabinet, or PIK3A Retro Gaming Table that can be found in this chapter.

< 98 >

3. Configure Your Controller

Take the newly updated SD card out of your computer and put it into your Pi. Plug in a USB controller, keyboard, and HDMI lead, and then attach the power cable to fire it up—RetroPie will run automatically.

The first time you do this, you'll have a chance to configure your game controller. You are actually taken to something called EmulationStation, which will be the front end through which you access RetroPie.

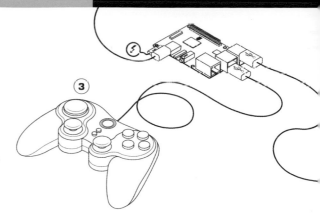

4. Install Your ROMs

Now, use your desktop computer or laptop to find the ROMs of the games you want to play. These are available all over the Internet, but you need to be sure that you are legally allowed to use the ROMs you download.

The easiest way to transfer your ROMs to RetroPie is to use a USB memory stick. Make sure the stick is formatted to FAT32 or NTFS and create a folder named "retropie" on your stick. Put the stick into your powered-up Pi, and wait for the lights to stop blinking: this will create a sub-folder named "roms." Remove the USB stick, and pop it into your computer. Copy your ROMs into the "roms" folder, under the game system the game file matches (there will be individual folders for each games system you can emulate).

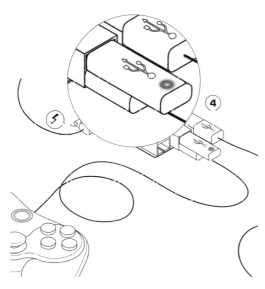

5. Play Your Games!

Once you've copied your ROMs to your USB stick, eject it from your computer and plug it back into your Pi. After the "active" light on the stick stops flashing (which may take some time), restart EmulationStation. All of your ROMs should now be available to play, listed under the game system they run on.

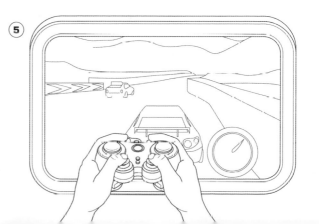

Build it! ➡️

Robust Minecraft® Server

Using a Raspberry Pi as a Minecraft
Server is a great way for you and your
friends to play the game together.

STATS

BUILDER	Daniel Lemire
TIME TO BUILD	One hour (depending on wait time)
COST TO BUILD	Approx. $50
DIFFICULTY	Intermediate

MATERIALS

→ Raspberry Pi

→ Ethernet cable

→ Case (optional)

→ Desktop or laptop computer (Windows or Mac)

The Project

Minecraft is primarily a creative tool, and creativity is often improved through collaboration. Joining friends online can make everything you build and discover in the game more fun and there are plenty of servers out there that you can join. However, what if you want to customize your experience with a particular blend of Minecraft mods and resource packs that no online server is currently providing? Or only want to play with certain people that you know? Or yearn to find out more about how Minecraft works under the hood?

In each of these cases, having your own personal Minecraft server is the answer. And the best news is that you don't need any specialist computer kit to do this—you can run a robust server on a Pi!

The Builder

Describing himself as a "techno-optimist," Daniel Lemire is a computer science professor at the University of Quebec, Canada, so he knows a thing or two about coding. Daniel's academic work isn't his only inspiration for coding projects, though. His children are keen gamers and devoted Minecraft fans, and when

Daniel saw the opportunity to build an accessible, reliable, and affordable Minecraft server for them, he jumped at the chance. The result is his Raspberry Pi-based Robust Minecraft Server.

TIPS

● Use an Ethernet cable. Even though it's possible to use a Wi-Fi connection, an Ethernet cable will make your server more reliable.

● This server is designed to be used with the Minecraft PC version of the game, rather than the Pi Edition (which already has a multiplayer option).

● Due to routers running a firewall between the Pi and the Internet, this server will only be accessible on your internal (home) network.

Get the code
quartoknows.com/page/raspberry-pi.

< 101 >

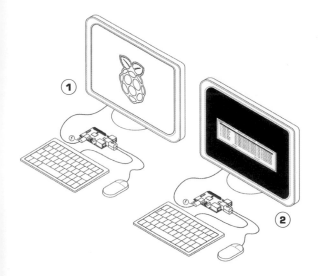

1. Set Up Your Pi

Make sure your Raspberry Pi is loaded with the latest version of Raspbian and connected to a monitor, mouse, keyboard, and power supply (see page 34).

Connect your Pi to your network using an Ethernet cable (see page 35). Be sure not to change the username of the Pi from its default ("pi").

Open a terminal window and enter the following command. This may take up more than one line in your terminal window, but it must be entered as a single line of text.

`sudo apt-get install netatalk screen avahi-daemon`

Press *Enter* and the command will install a handful of packages that are essential for your server. To confirm the installation has been successful, enter the command **`screen -list`** into the terminal—if you get the message "No Sockets found," all has gone well. If you are told there is no screen command you will need to repeat the previous install step.

2. Configuration Settings

Once the installation has been confirmed, open your Pi's configuration tool (using **`sudo raspi-config`**) and make these changes:

Expand FileSystem: This allows your Minecraft server to access the entire SD memory card.
Change Use Password: Change your Pi's password from the default ("raspberry").
Enable Boot to Desktop/Scratch: Choose Console Autologin so the Pi automatically logs in and doesn't boot to the desktop environment.
Internationalization Options: Configure your time and location.
Overclock: If this option is available, set the overclocking to maximum.
Advanced Options → Memory Split: Set the memory for the GPU to at least 16.
Advanced Options → SSH: Ensure that SSH server is enabled.

Exit the configuration tool, open a terminal window, type **`sudo reboot`**, and press *Enter* to reboot your Pi.

3. Go "Headless"

Now it's time to move to your main computer, which you'll connect to an SHH (Secure SHell). This allows a secure connection to another machine on the same network—in this case, your Raspberry Pi. Windows users should use a piece of software called PuTTY (available at www.putty.org) to access their Pi, while Mac users should enter **`ssh pi@raspberrypi.local`** into their computer's terminal.

You will now have remote access to your Pi via its "bash shell" and can unplug your Pi's monitor, keyboard, and mouse. The Pi is now running "headless." From the home directory on your Pi use the command **`mkdir minecraft && cd minecraft`** to build a directory where you will install your Minecraft files.

< 102 >

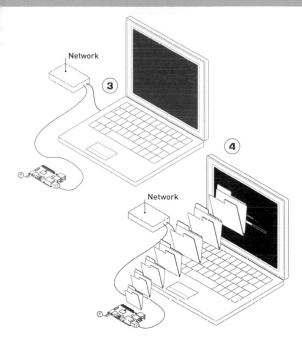

4. Build The Server

The server is going to be based on Spigot, which is a modified Minecraft server. You can get the build file for Spigot using the following single-line command (note that this should all be entered as a single line, even if the command runs across multiple lines in your browser):

wget https://hub.spigotmc. org/jenkins/job/BuildTools/ lastSuccessfulBuild/artifact/ target/BuildTools.jar

Once downloaded, you can build the server using the command **java -jar BuildTools.jar**.

After a long wait you should find several files have been created. Enter the command **ls spigot*.jar** to confirm the filename of your Spigot file. We're assuming a "1.9" file here, and this number is used in the commands in step 5. If you get a different number, don't worry—just replace "1.9" in the commands with your Spigot file number.

5. Start The Server

You can now fire up your server for the first time, using the command **java -jar -Xms512M -Xmx1008M spigot-1.9.jar nogui**. This will create a file called *eula.txt*. Open this file using the command **nano eula.txt** and edit it so it reads *eula=true*.

Run the server again (using **java -jar -Xms512M -Xmx1008M spigot-1.9.jar nogui** for a second time) and prepare yourself for another long wait. When the command prompt returns, your server will be operational.

6. Connect To Your Server

Run a game of Minecraft and connect to the server *raspberrypi.local* (on a Windows PC you first need to install "Bonjour Printer Services for Windows"). Verify that everything is working as it should and enter the final command: **stop**.

You've now built your own Minecraft server! To find out how to optimize and customize your server (and learn how to run it when it's not connected by SHH) visit Daniel's website: you'll find the details at the back of the book.

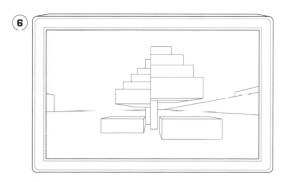

< 103 >

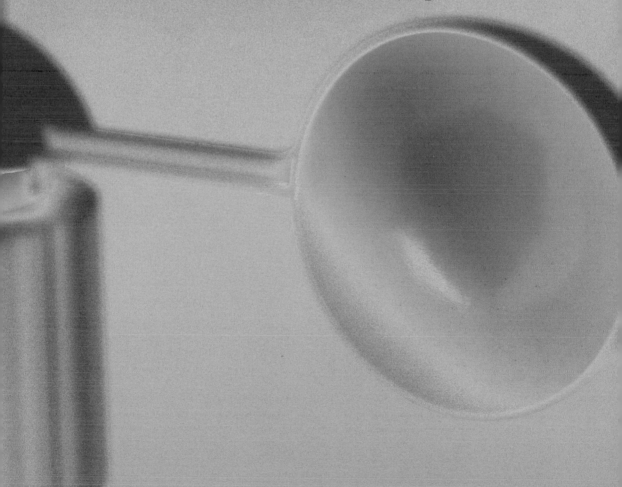

4

EXPERIMENTAL PI

Contribute to scientific progress from home

Batinator

The "Batinator" may look like a
creation from Dr Frankenstein's
laboratory, but it's an exceptionally
clever bat-watching device.

STATS

BUILDER	Martin Mander
TIME TO BUILD	Approx. 20 hours
COST TO BUILD	Approx. $90
DIFFICULTY LEVEL	Intermediate

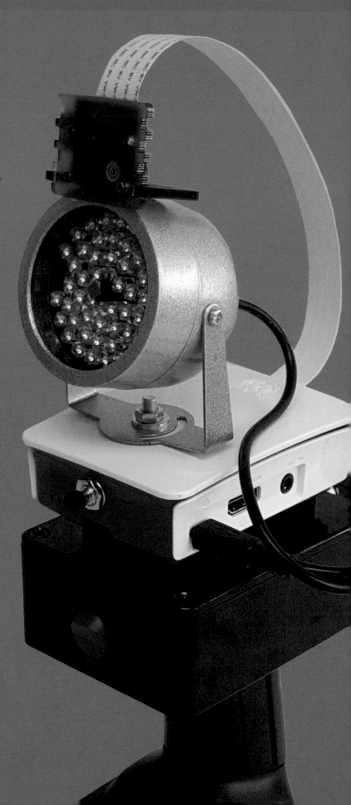

The Project

Like many great makers, Martin Mander pulled together a variety of elements to build his portable bat-watching device, or "Batinator," as he calls it.

At the bottom of the unit is the handle and battery from a 12-volt power drill, which not only provides power, but also makes the device easy to operate. To make it possible to "see in the dark" a Raspberry Pi and Pi NoIR camera module

The Batinator is pulled together from other tools, proving you don't always need specialist parts for an ambitious project.

are used in conjunction with a 48-LED infrared (IR) lamp: the lamp picks out the bats without giving off any visible light, while the specialist camera allows the Batinator to shoot up to two hours of video footage at an impressive 90 frames per second.

MATERIALS

→ Raspberry Pi 2
→ Pi NoIR camera module
→ USB Wi-Fi adaptor
→ Extended camera cable
→ 48-LED infrared illuminator
→ Short micro USB cable
→ Raspberry Pi case
→ Momentary push-to-make switch
→ Two jumper cables to connect the switch to the GPIO pins
→ Project box to house the 12V electrics
→ Rocker switch to control the power
→ 12V car socket
→ 12V-to-5V USB power adaptor
→ 12V cable plug
→ 12V battery powered drill

//

The Code

With a little trial and error, Martin managed to rework some camera-related code provided on *Average Man Vs Raspberry Pi*. You can use Martin's code directly, or go back to the original version that inspired him and try to rework it yourself: it might make the build tougher, but you're sure to learn a lot along the way.

//

< 107 >

From the coding to the construction, the Batinator is a relatively simple device that many eager builders should be able to reproduce quite easily, especially as Martin has provided detailed instructions online. However, there were plenty of challenges to overcome, especially when it came to making the Batinator fully portable and powerful enough to provide a good level of IR illumination.

The Builder

Martin has always had an interest in the world around him and is a regular Raspberry Pi builder—you can see his Internet Radio and Media Center projects on pages 148–151 and 166–171 respectively. So, when he wanted to learn more about bats, it made sense for him to call on Raspberry Pi technology to help him get a look at these remarkable flying mammals.

TIPS

● Test all the parts separately before putting them together: it's frustrating to complete an assembly and find out something has come loose or broken.

● Keep some switches pre-wired to jumper cables. This will make it easier to test the Pi's GPIO inputs, as you'll know a switch definitely works before you start.

● Make a large-scale printout of the Raspberry Pi's GPIO pinout diagram. It can be very helpful to have a pinout diagram stuck on the wall in front of you when your hands are juggling soldering equipment or your computer monitor is full of open windows displaying work-in-progress code.

It might not be pretty, but using hot glue to secure internal components can work incredibly well. Even some commercially sold gadgets use the technique.

An official Raspberry Pi case sits between the LED lamp and battery pack, protecting the Raspberry Pi.

< 108 >

An infrared LED array helps the Batinator's Pi NoIR camera module pick up flying rodents as they take to the skies come dusk.

How To Use This Idea

The Batinator is a great way of learning about the wildlife that takes over your garden, local park, or nearest countryside each night. You can also use many of the basic principles to start your own camera-based Pi project, such as a wildlife trap camera, motion-sensitive night-vision viewer, or spy camera.

< 109 >

SoilCam

SoilCam combines a Raspberry Pi
with a document scanner to produce
timelapse videos of the unseen world
beneath our feet.

STATS

BUILDER	Josh Williams
TIME TO BUILD	5–10 hours
COST TO BUILD	Approx. $100
DIFFICULTY LEVEL	Intermediate

MATERIALS

→ Raspberry Pi Model B
→ SD memory card
   (Class 10; 16–32GB)
→ Powered USB hub
→ Ethernet cable
→ Scanner
→ USB cable for scanner
→ Aquarium grade silicone
→ Rubbing alcohol
→ Microfiber cloth
→ Paper towels
→ Small shovel
→ Bucket

SoilCam is a great classroom project that uses technology to find out more about the natural world.

The Project

SoilCam is a waterproofed scanner buried slightly below the ground and connected to a Raspberry Pi. Every few minutes a scan is made of the earth in front of the scanner. At the end of each day a timelapse video is compiled automatically from these images and posted online.

The results are an amazing demonstration of just how interconnected life is. Soil is as important as water and is equally abundant in life, yet most of us are disconnected from what's happening in it: we can't see into it, so don't think of it as a three-dimensional space with plants and animals traversing it.

Josh's initial tests involved using a webcam and a fish tank, but this returned poor results. The challenge was to find a good lighting solution, and after talking with a number of people the idea of using a scanner came up. With its own lightsource, this was potentially ideal, although the scanner needed to be waterproofed (by sealing it with aquarium-grade

///

The Code

Programs written for the Linux operating system are often designed to send data from one program to another. The script for this project is highly efficient, as it can send data directly from the scanner program to the ImageMagick program.

///

< 111 >

silicone) and the earth around it had to be kept flat against the platen.

With this project, Josh learned a lot about the Raspberry Pi's Linux operating system, as well as how important soil is. It's great when technology can connect people to nature, especially when it's able to do so in a way that would be very difficult without that tech: to date more than one million people have seen Josh's "life of soil" timelapse videos.

Part of the success of the project comes from the Raspberry Pi's small size and quiet nature, which makes it ideal for running 24/7. Prior to using the small computer all of Josh's projects had laptops connected to them that were bulkier, used more electricity, and had fans that were just loud enough to remind you they were there.

If you plan on burying a scanner you need to make sure that any small gaps and holes are sealed.

The Builder

Josh Williams comes from Ann Arbor, MI, where he helps run maker spaces. When he's not helping people learn how to use various tools and technologies he can be found trying to catch up with his wife as she hikes, camps, and drives their growing family around the world.

TIPS

- If you want to make your own SoilCam, consider purchasing a used scanner. This not only saves money, but also helps reduce waste. However, you need to make sure the scanner is compatible with SANE (www.sane-project.org/sane-supported-devices.html).

- Consider where you are going to bury your scanner. If you bury it outside and power the scanner with a USB cable, this tends to have a limit of 25–30ft. You also need to check for access points, as the USB cable will need to run from the Pi inside your house to the scanner outside.

- If you plan on burying the scanner for more than a day, you need to seal any gaps or holes with aquarium-grade silicone. It's important you use this type of silicone, as it doesn't contain any anti-fungal chemicals that might impact the environment around the scanner.

Attaching a Raspberry Pi to a buried scanner can provide you with a window into a world that is rarely seen.

How To Use This Idea

Are you sure your bed is clean? Try placing your scanner face down on your sheets and have it record images for a day—the high-resolution scans will allow you to see small things you might not want to know about!

< 113 >

GroveWeatherPi

This modular weather station can be as simple or complex as you like, enabling it to be used for anything from a classroom project to a more in-depth scientific study.

STATS

BUILDER	John C. Shovic
TIME TO BUILD	Variable
COST TO BUILD	Variable
DIFFICULTY LEVEL	Intermediate

MATERIALS

Depending on what you want to
do with it, this project can use
a huge number of parts. Here's
some of the components you
will need, or could include:

→ Raspberry Pi

→ Pi2Grover

→ Weather board

→ Weather rack

→ Solar panels

→ Lightning sensor

//

The Code

There is a great deal of code for this project, but it is
all available from SwitchDoc Labs. To get this project
running, you'll need to add software and libraries to
your Raspberry Pi, such as MySQL and MatPlotLib (a
graphing subsystem with a great interface to Python).
The latter is a bit tricky to install, but there's an easy-to-
follow guide at the SwitchDoc website (switchdoc.com).

//

The Project

The GroveWeatherPi is, simply put, a connected, modular, solar-powered weather station designed by the SwitchDoc Labs team. It will let those that build it do a wide range of things, including sensing and recording wind speed, wind direction, rain, temperature, humidity, and barometric pressure, as well as detecting lightning. In addition to taking measurements, the GroveWeatherPi also builds a database of the environment it senses.

Although it may seem like an intimidating project, the team behind it has designed the weather station to be as simple as possible. At the heart of the project is the Grove system, which is a range of specialist boards that are linked via Grove Connectors, so there's no need for breadboards or soldering. You can get most of the components from the SwitchDoc Labs website, where you'll also find heaps of information and advice to help you with your build.

How To Use This Idea

Systems like this pack plenty of punch for their price, but you need to be prepared to cover potentially high costs. However, you might find you can inspire your school or a local science club to invest in the hardware—it makes a great teaching tool, which can provide years of quality learning.

The GroveWeatherPi can monitor both wind speed and direction.

< 116 >

Rainfall is another element that the GroveWeatherPi can record for you.

The GroveWeatherPi's solar panels allow you to measure and record sunlight levels.

< 117 >

The GroveWeatherPi includes almost everything needed to build a system that can monitor its environment.

The Builder

Dr. John C. Shovic has worked in industry for over 30 years, and has founded multiple companies. He has also served as a Professor of Computer Science at the University of Idaho, Eastern Washington University, and Washington State University. What's more, he has delivered 70 invited talks and has published over 50 papers on a variety of topics covering Arduino, Raspberry Pi, iBeacon, HIPAA, GLB, computer security, computer forensics, embedded systems, and related topics.

He is currently the CTO of SwitchDoc Labs, a software and hardware engineering company producing specialized products and designs for the small computer industry maker movement, and also holds a joint faculty position at the University of Idaho and North Idaho College as CS Program Manager, where he is devising a new Computer Science program. Yet despite all this, he still finds time to develop some remarkable Pi-powered projects, including the superb GroveWeatherPi!

< 118 >

A SunAirPlus Solar Power Controller converts the Raspberry Pi to solar power, which is ideal for outdoor installations like this.

TIPS

● Check your wiring multiple times before applying power. You don't want to cause yourself any problems through haste.

● There's an old saying heard in electronics workshops: "you can always trust your mother, but you can never trust your ground." If a project is giving you trouble, look for the loose or missing ground before you try anything else.

● If you are adding devices to any design, check to make sure the voltages are compatible with your existing system. If not, you could potentially "blow" your Raspberry Pi and the whole design!

< 119 >

Astro Pi

Astro Pi gave an international team of astronauts all the tools it needed to conduct out-of-this world experiments. There's no reason why you can't emulate their adventures with your own Raspberry Pi.

STATS

BUILDER	Various
TIME TO BUILD	Several hours (+ time designing experiments to upload)
COST TO BUILD	Approx. $130 (excluding a space-grade flight case and launching the project into space...)
DIFFICULTY LEVEL	Intermediate (unless you want to build that space-grade flight case...)

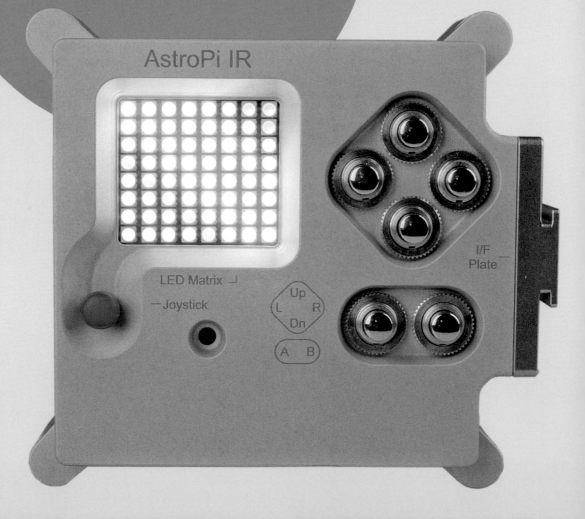

Adding a Sense HAT lets
your Raspberry Pi "read"
the world around it.

The Project

At the end of 2015, the Principia mission saw ESA astronaut Tim Peake blast off to the International Space Station (ISS) to carry out a range of experiments that were not possible down here on Earth. However, the experiments on board weren't just commissioned by space agencies and professional researchers. Thanks to a very special Raspberry Pi project, several experiments that formed part of the Principia mission were designed and coded by schoolchildren.

Astro Pi saw two Raspberry Pis sent into space ahead of the mission crew, packed with

MATERIALS

→ Raspberry Pi Model B+
→ Sense HAT
→ Raspberry Pi camera module or an infrared camera (Pi NoIR)
→ Flight case (unavailable to buy, and wildly expensive, but you can download 3D printing plans for your own version at rpf.io/aptc)

//

The Code
You can download all the code from the Principia mission at astro-pi.org/principia/science-results.

//

< 121 >

experiments that Peake would undertake while orbiting the planet on the ISS.

Of course, the two Pis on board the space station were not just free-floating bare boards. Firstly, each was coupled with a Sense HAT, which adds a gyroscope, an accelerometer, a magnetometer sensor, temperature and humidity sensors, a barometric pressure sensor, a simple LED display, and a mini joystick to a standard Pi. A regular camera module was then added to one Pi, and a Pi NoIR infrared camera added to the other.

A hugely expensive flight case also needed to be designed, not only to house the Astro Pi, but to make sure the hardware met the demanding safety standards required of any experiment going into space. As a slight variance in surface temperature or a sharp edge could cause havoc in the

The Astro Pi's space-grade enclosure might be one of the most expensive custom Pi cases ever made. You can use a 3D printer to recreate your own version of this project, but the case isn't essential.

depths of space, this element
had to be extremely precise in
its design and manufacture.

Thankfully, it is fairly easy
to build your own "domestic
Astro Pi," as demonstrated by
the Sensor Station on pages
130–133.

No matter what case you use,
you need to make sure that
the Raspberry Pi's ports
remain accessible.

How To Use This Idea

For some people, building a version of real space hardware will be enough
to make it worth tackling an Astro Pi build. More than that, you can use the
Astro Pi to further your understanding of the diverse abilities of the Sense
HAT board, and to get to grips with what both visible light and infrared
cameras can offer Raspberry Pi projects. You can also start coding
software that could one day be used out in space!

< 123 >

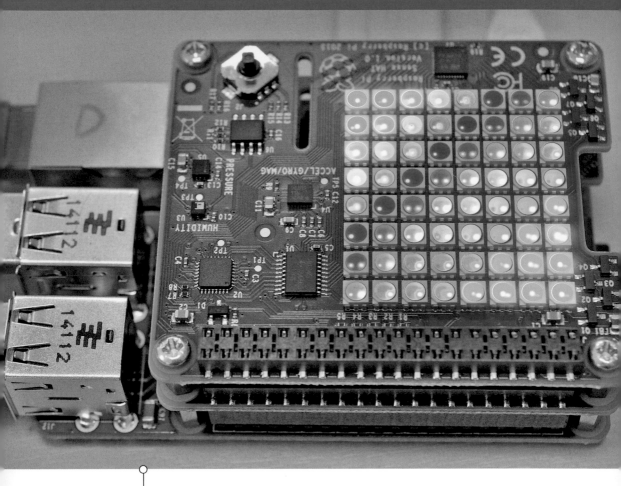

The Sense HAT's LED display is a simple, yet effective, means of communication.

The Builder

James Adams, Jonathan Bell, and David Honess were the principal designers of the hardware for the Astro Pi initiative, but they are just three of many people who brought this project to life: teams from the European Space Agency, the UK Space Agency, and the Raspberry Pi Foundation all worked hard to make Astro Pi a reality.

Technology partners including Airbus Defense & Space, CGI, Surrey Satellite Technology, QinetiQ, and UK Space also pitched in a considerable effort, while organizations such as Esero, KTN, and Nesta helped with the education and outreach element of the Astro Pi project's success.

Finally, there were ordinary schoolchildren of many ages who shaped the experiments that were loaded onto a launch vehicle with the hardware, before being propelled beyond our atmosphere.

< 124 >

The Sense HAT is designed specifically for the Raspberry Pi, and simply clips onto the top, attaching to the GPIO.

TIPS

- Even though it won't make it into space directly, building your own Astro Pi will help you prototype experiment ideas for the real thing. Why is that important? Because there may be plenty of other chances to send Earth-written code to the Astro Pis aboard the ISS.

- Astro Pi makes a great classroom project, as it can get children deeply engaged in learning. Some young coders have even been known to stay late at school voluntarily, just because they have become so involved in the project!

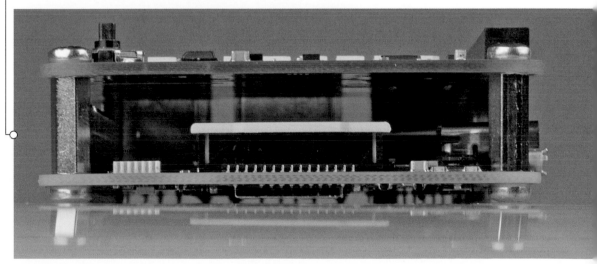

< 125 >

PocketCluster

Multiplying the power of Pi by six (or more) will let you create your very own PocketCluster—a low-cost "supercomputer" that's capable of tackling heavyweight applications.

STATS

BUILDER	Sung-Taek Kim
TIME TO BUILD	This builder had "too much fun" to count the hours!
COST TO BUILD	Approx. $300
DIFFICULTY LEVEL	Intermediate–Advanced

You'll need multiple Raspberry Pis to make a PocketCluster, but it is still one of the most affordable ways to build your own supercomputer.

MATERIALS

→ 6 x Raspberry Pi 2 Model B+
→ 6 x SD memory cards (8GB)
→ 6 x 12" Ethernet cables
→ 6 x 12" 90-degree right-angled micro USB to USB Type A cables
→ Six-port 50W+ USB charger
→ Eight-port network switch
→ Custom PocketCluster case
→ 2 x M3 hex nuts
→ 22 x M3 x 25mm pillar screws
→ 4 x M3 whirled hex nuts
→ 6 x M3 x 4mm screws
→ 24 x M2.5 x 5mm screws
→ 24 x M2.5 hex nuts
→ 24 x M2.5 x 5mm pillar screws

The Project

In the simplest sense, the PocketCluster combines six Pi units to make a "supercomputer" that can analyze large amounts of data and train models to learn from such an analysis. It also provides an environment in which users can learn from experience and conduct edgy experiments. In other words, it's an affordable supercomputer that scales up the Raspberry Pi's spirit of accessible computing.

The inspiration to build the PocketCluster came when Sung-Taek Kim was conducting analysis research on a large amount of data from buildings. The technological environment he was working in simply wasn't as flexible as he had hoped for, so he began considering alternatives.

Around the same time, the Raspberry Pi 2 was freshly released and Microsoft had announced Windows 10 support. Sung-Taek began to consider how the Pi 2 might be able to help with his research, and threw together a test

//

The Code

Building your own PocketCluster is a code- and software-intensive project. You'll certainly need to use Python; getting to grips with Scala will be useful; there's a little bit of Java to learn; and you will likely have to familiarize yourself with the MapReduce programming model as well.

//

< 127 >

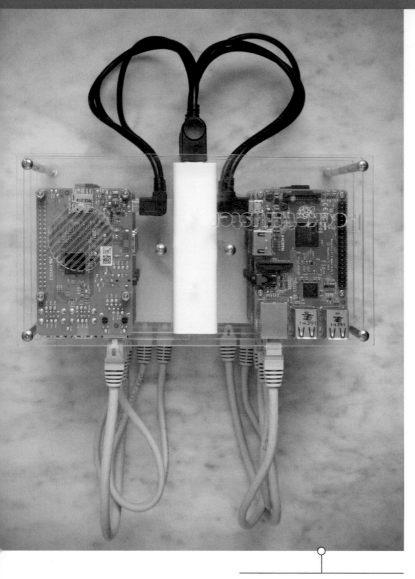

cluster. It not only worked brilliantly, but also provided the exact environment its builder was seeking.

Although Raspberry Pi projects are often considered to be more playful than serious, this is certainly not the case with this creation. With a single cluster, the creative mind behind it (who is also something of a data scientist) has performed a host of experiments that he was previously unable to tackle. PocketCluster has enabled him to test ideas close to what he labels "insanity," and has helped him gain numerous insights into big data and machine learning.

Just as the PocketCluster offers strength through the number of Raspberry Pis used, so the project has grown as new builders try their own version. Describing that process with the language of data science, Sung-Taek reveals he has had his joy "tremendously amplified" by seeing others join the PocketCluster project.

You can make a PocketCluster case from almost anything: Sung-Taek chose acrylic.

How To Use This Idea

A supercomputer is defined as a machine with many times the computational power of its more common contemporaries. Using Sung-Taek's basic principles you could use a cluster to do any number of things beyond the power of a single Raspberry Pi. The possibilities might not be truly endless, but a project of this type could certainly give you the capacity to crunch some serious data!

< 128 >

The Builder

Sung-Taek Kim is a software engineer who has built one of the most powerful Raspberry Pi projects there is.

Yet although Sung-Taek is something of an expert in the field of handling big data, his first experiment with the Raspberry Pi was rather less specialized: working with a Model B+, he got the iconic first-person shooter video game, *Quake*, up and running, purely to test the Raspberry Pi's prowess.

Since then, he has largely devoted his time with the hardware to building pure software projects, although on occasion he will craft something that combines software and hardware in a way where one cannot function without the other. A recent example is Sung-Taek's aviation-positioning simulator, which employs multiple Raspberry Pi boards that can accurately imitate conditions around an airport.

TIPS

● The cluster in this project is offered as an example, not an instruction. It isn't necessary to build an identical case, or to have the exact same number of nuts: you can readily build a cluster with off-the-shelf components, for example.

● In theory, there is no limit to the number of Pis you can have in a cluster: you could reduce the number to cut costs, or use more if you want to boost performance.

As with most Raspberry Pi projects, determining how you will access the various ports (and their ideal position) is an important part of the design process.

An "open" case like this will leave the Raspberry Pis exposed to the elements, but it keeps things lightweight, affordable, is relatively uncomplicated, and provides easy access.

< 129 >

Sensor Station

A few simple steps is all it takes to transform a Raspberry Pi into an Astro Pi-style Sensor Station that can be used to monitor temperature, air pressure, and more!

STATS

BUILDER	Craig Hissett
TIME TO BUILD	1 hour
COST TO BUILD	Approx. $90
DIFFICULTY LEVEL	Beginner

MATERIALS

→ Raspberry Pi 3
(Model B+ or 2 also usable)

→ Sense HAT

→ Case with a clear top that
can accommodate the Pi
and the HAT

→ 8GB micro SD card

→ Card reader (for flashing
OS to SD card)

→ Ethernet cable

→ 5V power supply

→ Keyboard and monitor
for local setup

The Project

The key component in building a Sensor Station is a Sense HAT. This is an add-on board that comes with an array of sensors and an 8 x 8 LED matrix for displaying scrolling messages. It also has a Python library written for it already.

Not only can you report the Sense HAT's findings via a scrolling LED message, but Wi-Fi enables you to wirelessly transmit the information to a web page using a Python web server, so you can access the data from anywhere on your home network.

The Builder

Craig Hissett is an admin assistant at a college in the north east of England. Alongside his job he's studying for a Foundation Degree in Business and Administrative Systems, and hopes to one day work in a systems/software development role.

TIPS

● The Sense HAT comes with a number of spacers that can be fitted between it and the Raspberry Pi. If your case allows it, it's a good idea to fit the spacers, to ensure your Sense HAT is level and secure.

● The Raspberry Pi 3 has built-in Wi-Fi, but you could also use a different Raspberry Pi version with a compatible Wi-Fi dongle.

● Any commands you enter into the terminal are case sensitive, so type them carefully to avoid introducing any errors.

How To Use This Idea

With the addition of a portable 5V power bank you could place this project anywhere, while tweaking the code would enable you to expand it in a number of directions: you could add more sensors, for example; have more data relayed; log the recorded data to the Pi's micro SD card or a USB memory stick; or even have your Pi record data to an "Internet of Things" site.

Get the code
quartoknows.com/page/raspberry-pi

< 131 >

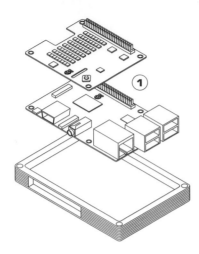

1. Attach The Sense HAT

Before you begin you'll need a freshly installed and updated operating system on your Pi. Then, line up the Sense HAT's female header with the Pi's GPIO pins and gently push the Sense HAT down to attach it to the Pi.

To keep things neat, you can put the Pi and Sense HAT in a case, but it's worth noting that the heat generated by the Pi's CPU can lead to slightly high readings, especially if the case is closed up. (For greater accuracy you can connect the Sense HAT to the Pi using a ribbon cable, which enables the sensors to be distanced from the Pi.)

With the Pi up and running, you need to install the Tornado Library. This will run the web server part of the code, so you can read the values recorded by the Pi anywhere on your home network. To install the Tornado Library, open the terminal and type:

```
install tornado (sudo pip3 install tornado)
```

2. Add Your Code

To run your code correctly, you need to set up three folders using the terminal and the "mkdir" command:

```
mkdir /home/pi/PiSenseHat
mkdir /home/pi/PiSenseHat/templates
mkdir /home/pi/PiSenseHat/static/js
```

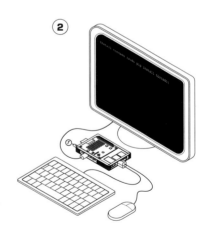

With the folders in place you can create your code files using the Nano text editor. Enter **sudo nano /home/pi/ PiSenseHat/server.py** and copy the *server.py* code from the website. When you've finished, press *Ctrl + X* to exit Nano. You will be prompted to save the file by pressing *Y*.

Next, enter **sudo nano /home/pi/PiSenseHat/SenseScript.py** and copy the *SenseScript.py* code from the website. Close and save the file as before.

Repeat the process with **sudo nano /home/pi/PiSenseHat/templates/index.html** and the *index.html* code from the website. Finally, enter **sudo nano /home/pi/PiSenseHat/ static/js/ jquery-2.2.0.min.js** and copy the *jquery-2.2.0.min.js* code from the website. In both cases, save the file and exit Nano.

< 132 >

3. Launch On Startup

Once the code has been added you can set it to run on startup. This is great if you're running the sensor station in a location that isn't easily accessible.

Open the *rc.local* file in Nano by typing **sudo nano /etc/rc.local**. Add the following commands to run before the *exit 0* line. The first command runs the script that controls the Sense HAT's scrolling screen and the second triggers your web server:

```
sudo python3 /home/pi/PiSenseHat/SenseScript.py &
sudo python3 /home/pi/PiSenseHat/server.py &
```

When you've entered the code press *Ctrl + X* then *Y*, followed by *Enter* to save the file. Reboot your Raspberry Pi using **sudo reboot** and your sensor station should be up and running automatically!

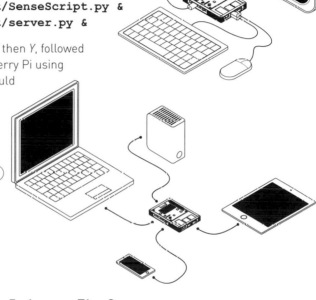

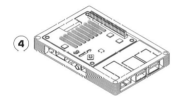

4. Check The Display

There are two display elements to this project. The first is a scrolling display on the Sense HAT. This should start to run 10–15 seconds after the Raspberry Pi is powered up. If not, check the command entered in the previous step: the code is case sensitive and shouldn't feature any incorrect spaces.

The second display element is a web server that will allow you to view the data on any device connected to your network, such as a computer or smartphone. To do this you need to know the Raspberry Pi's IP address, which you can find by opening the terminal and typing:

sudo ifconfig

5. Access The Server

The previous command will list the network information for your Pi: the Wi-Fi information is listed as *wlan0*, and the IP address appears next to *inet addr.*

To access the web server, open a web browser window on your networked device (your computer, tablet, or smartphone) and type the Raspberry Pi's IP address into the address bar, adding **:8000** at the end (this signifies port 8000, which is the port that the Raspberry Pi's web server is running on). This will bring up a simple page displaying the readings from your Sensor Station: clicking on the button on the page will update the readings.

< 133 >

5

HOME PI
Smart devices for the automated home

Movie Player

A Pi-based movie player makes a great in-car entertainment system that is guaranteed to keep the kids occupied when you're on the go.

STATS

BUILDER	Craig Hissett
TIME TO BUILD	70 hours
COST TO BUILD	Approx. $90
DIFFICULTY LEVEL	Beginner

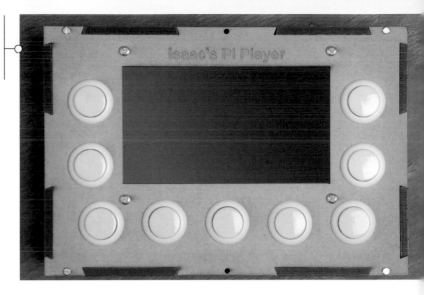

The movie player's large buttons are much easier for young children to use than a touchscreen, and also harder to break!

MATERIALS

→ Raspberry Pi Model B
→ 9 x arcade style buttons
→ ELI70-CR 7" touchscreen
→ Powered USB hub
→ 2.5" portable hard drive
→ Adafruit Powerboost 1000C
→ 4 x 18650 batteries
→ Case
→ Hookup wire
→ HDMI splitter

The Project

Like many children, Craig's son has an extensive collection of DVDs that he loves to watch all the time. However, whenever he goes to his grandparents' house he has to leave his movies at home—and as they don't have a USB port on their TV he can't play them from USB sticks either. Luckily, Craig had been looking for a project to make for his son, and a movie player ticked all the right boxes.

Craig's plan was to create a box that his son could take with him with all his media on it. The player needed to have a simple interface that would let his son choose what he wanted to watch, so the device not only features a touchscreen, but also nine arcade-style buttons that allow category and movie selection and act as standard play, pause, and skip controls. These two control methods mean that children and adults of all ages can use the device.

//

The Code

Craig's movie player uses tboplayer by github user KenT2. This piece of software is Python based, has a simple interface, is well documented, and doesn't require too many libraries to run, which made it ideal for the project. Craig simply added a line of code to make it run on startup.

//

< 137 >

The main issue with the build was powering the device: no matter how "right" it looked on paper, Craig kept burning out his powerboost circuitry. After several rewires and replacement boards the player started to work as planned, but to this day Craig's still not sure what the problem was!

The Builder

Craig Hissett is a College Administrative Assistant from Newcastle upon Tyne in the north east of England. Having always had an interest in writing code, Craig has created a few Microsoft Access databases in his career and was keen to learn additional languages to VBA (Visual Basic for Applications).

Being a bit of a geek at heart, he was keen to start turning his many ideas into real-life products. However, as hardware and electronics were not his strength, he started out with the Arduino, before learning to write code in Python and moving to the Raspberry Pi platform.

There are countless LCD touchscreens that are compatible with the Raspberry Pi, but you will need to balance your preferred screen size and resolution with your budget.

How To Use This Idea

Arcade buttons provide a simple way of navigating the movie player. The nine buttons are wired to a GPIO pin and 5V power supply, with a simple script detecting button presses. However, all that's really needed to make a great portable player is a Raspberry Pi, a touchscreen, and a power source.

Craig used laser-cut MDF for his case, which gives the movie player a simple yet robust housing.

< 138 >

TIPS

- Plan, plan, and plan again! Having a goal is great, but think about how to get there so the project takes less time to put together.

- Research your materials. You can waste a lot of time and money ordering parts that aren't fit for purpose: sometimes the cheapest parts are not the best option.

- A major stumbling block with this project was powering it: having 12V and 5V devices powered from the same source led to a lot of problems, destroying components and batteries in the process. If you have differing voltages make sure you plan to power them correctly and adequately.

Clickity-Clank: Smart Piggy Bank

Whether you need to save money to finance a project, go on vacation, or something else entirely, a Pi-powered piggy bank will help you achieve your goal.

STATS

BUILDER	Roberto Pigliacelli
TIME TO BUILD	10 hours
COST TO BUILD	Approx. $135
DIFFICULTY LEVEL	Beginner

A smart piggy bank is a great way to save up to buy more electronics to make things with!

MATERIALS

→ Raspberry Pi Model B+
→ GrovePi+
→ Wi-Fi dongle
→ Power supply for Pi
→ 3V power supply for DC motor
→ Grove LCD RGB backlight
→ Grove button
→ Grove red LED
→ Grove green LED
→ Grove rotary angle sensor
→ Grove buzzer
→ 2 x generic relay NC/NO 5V PIC ARM AVR D
→ 1K Ohm resistor
→ 10k Ohm resistor
→ Jumpers
→ DVD player lens mechanism
→ LEGO® DUPLO® blocks and base
→ Small screws for relay and Grove sensors
→ Medium screws with washers for DVD lens mechanism
→ Knob

The Project

When Roberto was younger, he had a "piggy bank" to save his coins in, so he had money to buy video games. However, his "bank" was just a plastic bottle, so it was hard to know when he had saved enough.

Fast-forward to today and Roberto no longer needs to check how much he's got, because every time he inserts a coin into Clickity-Clank he's sent an email update with a graph showing how much money has been saved in total. He can set a target amount, decide how many days he has to reach the target, and his "smart" piggy bank will tell him when the goal's been reached.

Since revealing the project, people have pointed out that it is a great way of introducing children to electronics and coding. This is helped by his use of a GrovePi+ board kit, which makes putting together the electronics quite easy.

//

The Code

A Python script does much of the work in the piggy bank, but a Bash script is needed to set the parameters to draw a graph and save it as a .PNG file.

//

< 141 >

How To Use This Idea

You can invert the polarity of a DC motor by using a couple of NO/NC relays. This allows you to make continuous and repeated movements of a mechanism.

Clickity-Clank is a great classroom project that not only teaches children about coding, but also encourages them to save their money!

The Builder

Roberto Pigliacelli initially started writing programs using Microsoft Visual Basic, but found it difficult to understand for a first-time coder. He then came across Raspberry Pi, which he describes as perfect: the platform had a lot of open-source code that he could copy, modify, and paste to create something new.

Since then, Roberto has also learned how to use the Arduino platform, which he says is more versatile, but harder to understand. After his first few projects, Roberto has dedicated his attention to creating projects with "real world" uses, many of which are running in his home.

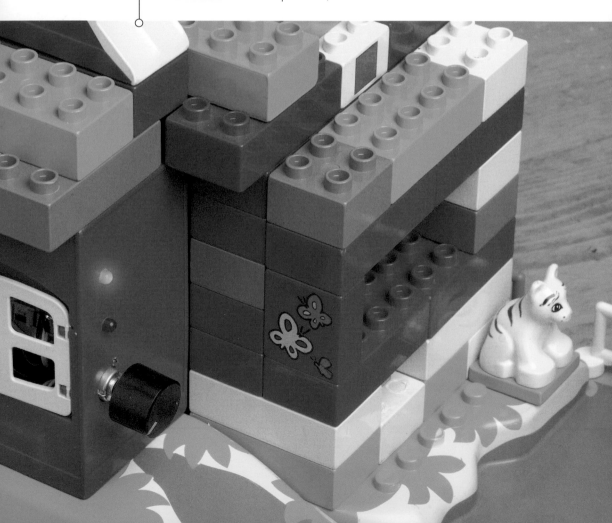

TIPS

● The two relays used in the circuit can be replaced by an H-bridge (IC L239D).

● The Grove components can be replaced with a more conventional circuit consisting of a momentary switch, a rotary encoder, LEDs, and a buzzer.

Make sure your design allows you to access your Pi's connectors so you can check them without taking the whole bank apart.

< 143 >

Internet Monitor

"Is the Internet down?" is a common cry around the world, but with this project you'll be able to see your connection status at a glance.

STATS

BUILDER	Bruce Hillsberg
TIME TO BUILD	40 hours
COST TO BUILD	Approx. $150
DIFFICULTY LEVEL	Intermediate

MATERIALS

→ Raspberry Pi (any version)

→ ⅜" thick birch plywood (16" x 16")

→ Industrial safety tower lamp (red/yellow/green)

→ 16mm illuminated red push-button momentary switch

→ Half-sized Perma-Proto Raspberry Pi breadboard

The Project

Bruce Hillsberg had a simple mission: to use a Raspberry Pi to make a device that monitored the Internet and could tell anybody what the current status of their local connection was. However, he also wanted to be sure that his device would look great. After all, most people don't want to have a mess of exposed wires and bare circuit boards decorating their home.

The result is Bruce's Internet Monitor, which sports a distinctly industrial look that wouldn't be out of place in many homes. It also serves a very practical purpose and offers a great conversation piece that often reveals visitors have plans for their own Raspberry Pi projects.

However, building the Internet Monitor wasn't without its challenges. For a start, Bruce had to create a Python program that would reliably check the status of the Internet connection. Without that working, the Internet Monitor might become as unreliable as Bruce's own wireless connection, and that would be no good. He also had to meticulously design the laser-cut case so it would neatly house the Raspberry Pi.

//

The Code

Starting from scratch would make the Internet Monitor a fairly complex coding challenge, but Bruce has made everything available online. On his Instructables page (see page 218) you'll find a detailed guide to the code and terminal commands you'll need to enter, along with ways to get your Raspberry Pi to employ special Python programs, and how to configure it to your wireless Internet connection.

//

The effort was worth it, though. The finished project uses a tower lamp that shows green if the Internet connection is reliable, amber if it is misbehaving a little, and red if it's down. The project also features an illuminated switch that indicates when the monitor is operational (and will shut down the Raspberry Pi when pressed); a barrier strip for connecting the circuit board to the tower lamp; and jacks for hooking things up. All in all, it's an impressive, detailed, and practical build.

The Builder

Calling Silicon Valley home, Bruce Hillsberg is based in the epicenter of the technology universe. He loves experimenting with new technologies and has been making, taking things apart, and repurposing them since he was a middle-school student.

Bruce is a regular at his local maker space, "TechShop," which not only provides him with access to specialist tools such as a laser cutter, but enables him to meet other project builders with whom he can share ideas and advice. There are maker spaces all over the world, and it's worth checking if there is one in your area—if there is, it might just help you make your next project as impressive as Bruce's Internet Monitor.

How To Use This Idea

Replicating Bruce's project will not only give you a fantastically useful home gadget, but it will also teach you a lot about how your Raspberry Pi interfaces with the Internet. It's also a great lesson in building brilliant-looking enclosures and you'll certainly absorb a thing or two about using the Python language as well.

< 146 >

The Internet monitor is fitted with a simple shutdown button, similar to the project featured on pages 44-47.

TIPS

- When you're developing Python code for a project, search online to find examples of code from other people that does something similar to what you want to achieve. It's often easier to modify and experiment with existing code, and it's also a great way to hone your programming skills.

- If you plan on using a laser cutter to make an enclosure it's a good idea to build a card version first. Cutting card with a knife is faster and cheaper than using wood or acrylic and a laser cutter, and reduces waste while you hone the design.

- Learn how to debug the software for your projects before mounting your Pi and electronics into an enclosure. This will eliminate the need to disassemble the project if you need to access the SD card or rewire any components.

An industrial tower lamp tells you in an instant if your Internet connection is up or down.

Internet Radio

Martin Mander's Internet Radio brings
a 21st-century audio experience to an
iconic 1970s design.

STATS

BUILDER	Martin Mander
TIME TO BUILD	45 hours
COST TO BUILD	Approx. $100
DIFFICULTY LEVEL	Intermediate

MATERIALS

- → 1979 Bang & Olufsen Beocord 1500 cassette recorder
- → Raspberry Pi 1 Model B+
- → Wi-Fi adaptor
- → Sugru
- → Adafruit RGB Negative 16x2 LCD kit
- → Celcus soundbar
- → 10 x lever microswitches
- → AD557 DAC (Digital-to-Analog Convertor) integrated circuit
- → Color-changing LEDs
- → Jumper cables
- → Ribbon cable and GPIO cobbler breakout board
- → Meccano
- → Perspex photo frame
- → 2-way electrical extension socket
- → Roofing bolts

The Project

Martin Mander loves vintage technology and often builds projects based around the classic tech he finds in yard sales. The starting point for this particular build was a broken Bang & Olufsen cassette recorder that Martin wanted to transform into an Internet radio.

Bang & Olufsen stereos from the 1970s have an iconic look, and Martin wanted to retain all of its style. It was important that the analog VU meters

The Code

Martin's Internet Radio uses an Adafruit LCD screen and push buttons, but there are several other code options available to support inputs such as rotary dials and different screens. This may make it worth working in reverse and choosing the case for your radio first, before deciding on the code to use!

< 149 >

remained functional, so he drove these using the Raspberry Pi and a DAC (digital-to-analog convertor).

However, in a nod to modernity, the current time, station, and track are displayed on an Adafruit RGB Negative display, which is visible through what was originally the cassette window. The radio also features a color-changing mood LED that projects through the tape counter window.

Amplification is provided by a repurposed TV soundbar

built into the front of the case. Although there's a remote control for the amplifier built into a cassette tape, Martin's favorite part of the radio is the way that it's controlled using the original buttons. This was also the hardest thing to get working—Martin initially used lever microswitches, but it was difficult to get them lined up and working properly without them wobbling too much. In the end he added small wooden braces to hold them steady—a simple solution, but a workable one.

How To Use This Idea
Whether you plan on making a radio or something else, most projects can benefit from some cool mood lighting! This project uses simple, color-changing LEDs run from the Raspberry Pi's 5V output.

Martin was adamant that he wanted to use the cassette recorder's original analog VU meters in his modern radio.

< 150 >

When it first appeared, the Internet Radio got a great reaction, not only from the Raspberry Pi community, but also from hi-fi purists; Martin even got a nice Tweet from Bang & Olufsen!

The Builder

Martin Mander is a Raspberry Pi and retro technology fanatic from Norwich, in the UK. He built his first Raspberry Pi project in 2014 and has been an enthusiast ever since, finding the platform to be the perfect blend of size, capability, and accessibility. Working on the Pi reminds

Martin of the hours he spent as a child typing code from magazines into Commodore VIC-20 and Sinclair ZX81 computers, although you can do so much more with a Raspberry Pi!

The Internet Radio was only Martin's second Pi project (after his Media Center on pages 166–171), so he was still finding his way around the technology and honing his soldering skills. Since then he's created several more projects, including the AlexaPhone and the RabbitPi.

The Internet Radio utilizes the original controls, but this required a little bit of ingenuity to implement.

TIPS

- Meccano is a great tool for prototyping and is ideal when a project needs a semi-permanent bracket or structure. Meccano comes in different sizes and can be bent to just the right shape.

- If you're building something structural and get stuck for materials, take a trip to your local hardware store. There are countless different fixtures and fittings, and very often you can make use of something you would not have considered otherwise.

- If a part doesn't seem to work, check everything else before re-soldering. When his LCD screen didn't appear to be working, Martin re-soldered the connections three times before realizing the screen's contrast setting was wrong!

< 151 >

Coffee Roaster

Nothing beats the smell of fresh-roast
coffee, so why not put a Pi-powered roaster
on your project list?

STATS

BUILDER	Mark Sanders
TIME TO BUILD	60 hours
COST TO BUILD	Approx. $100
DIFFICULTY LEVEL	Intermediate

The coffee roaster's spacious housing ensures there's room for the Raspberry Pi and all of the other necessary components.

MATERIALS

- → Raspberry Pi
- → Raspberry Pi power supply
- → Raspberry Pi breakout board
- → Type K thermocouple
- → Thermocouple amplifier MAX31855 breakout board
- → AC relay
- → NPN transistor
- → AC outlet (and box to contain it)
- → Popcorn popper
- → 2 x red LEDs
- → 2 x yellow LEDs
- → 10ft AC power cord
- → 10K Ohm resistor
- → 4 x 300 Ohm resistors
- → Wooden box
- → Black spray paint
- → Wire

The Project

It was Mark's pursuit of delicious coffee that led him to start roasting his own beans at home. He started out using a popcorn popper, but found that it roasted the coffee too quickly. This meant he had to continually unplug it and plug it back in to control the roast, which wasn't ideal.

Discussing this problem with his co-workers, someone suggested using a Raspberry Pi to control the temperature. After some research, Mark had identified the parts he would need and his coffee roaster now consists of a popcorn popper, plus an AC relay, a thermocouple, some LEDs, and a Raspberry Pi.

The Raspberry Pi controls the temperature inside the popper using a thermocouple to measure the temperature and an AC relay to control the heater. The software measures

< 153 >

The coffee roaster monitors and regulates the temperature of the popcorn popper to ensure the perfect roast. To achieve this, a Raspberry Pi (1) is connected to a fairly complex circuit (2), with a solid state relay (SSR) boosting the power to the heater (3).

the temperature every 0.1 seconds, and depending on the measurement, turns the heater on or off.

The software also logs the temperature during the roast for review at a later time, using a retro-industrial custom web interface that was also created by Mark.

The biggest challenge was the electrical aspects of the project. Mark had to learn about relays and transistors in order to control the heater on the popper. This was also Mark's first time soldering electrical components—a learning experience that has tripped up many of the makers in this book! It took several attempts and plenty of online

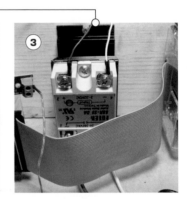

With its base removed, the popcorn popper's heater was revealed. Mark hooked it up to an AC relay that cycles the power to the heater on and off to control the temperature of the roast.

< 154 >

soldering videos before Mark was soldering reliably.

Since he published his project online, Mark has received emails from people all over the world who are attempting to build their own roasters. Some are experienced developers, but most are people who are just learning about the Raspberry Pi and its software.

//

The Code

It took a while for Mark to create the temperature gauge in his custom web interface. He did it by creating a Python script that overlaid the needle on the gauge background and rotated it in 5-degree increments, saving a new image at every increment. All of these images are downloaded to the web browser when the web page first loads. The web page changes the image every second when it gets the latest information about the roast from the Raspberry Pi, which gives the impression of the needle moving.

//

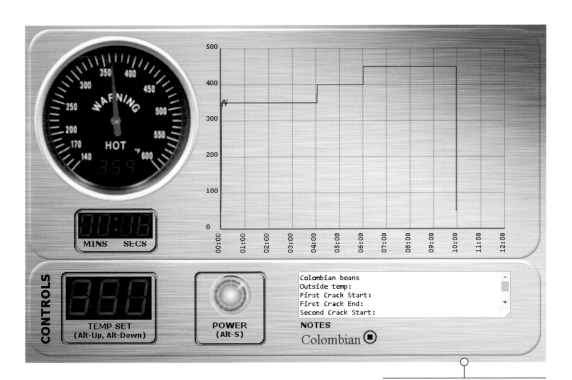

Mark's custom web interface enables him to monitor the roast and record the details for future reference.

< 155 >

At the core of the coffee roaster is a popcorn popper, which Mark found for sale at a thrift store.

The Builder

Mark Sanders has a degree in Mechanical Engineering, a master's degree in Computer Science, and has been a software developer for 20 years, during which time he has worked on military radios, business phone systems, and warehousing systems. He programs mainly in C/C++, but recently learned Django and Python to do some web-based programming.

It was a co-worker who first mentioned the Raspberry Pi to Mark and he was immediately amazed at how affordable the unit was given its capabilities. Most appealing was that it ran Linux, which he was already familiar with. When he was looking for a web interface for this project, Mark knew he could run a web server on Linux, which is not possible with some of the other small, single-board computers.

How To Use This Idea

There is nothing in the user interface or code that makes this project specifically about roasting coffee: it can be used for any project that requires temperature control. The AC relay circuit design and code can be used to control any device that plugs into an AC outlet, such as a fan or heater, so you might modify it for beer making, a kiln, an oven, and so on.

< 156 >

TIPS

- When connecting a ribbon cable to the Raspberry Pi's GPIO header, make sure you connect it the right way around. With this project you will damage the thermocouple board if you connect the cable incorrectly. Mark spent several hours troubleshooting before he realized his mistake!

- Whenever a project requires a substantial amount of code, use a software version control system to help manage the source code files. This makes it easy to identify changes between versions of files, backup source files, and create branches for developing different features. It can also help speed up any debugging.

- Take lots of pictures! Mark took lots of photographs of the roaster to make sure he could rewire and reassemble it correctly. He also took pictures of the breadboard connections before he tried a new circuit, so if the circuit didn't work he had a visual reference to take him back to the previous design.

You don't have to design an awesome container like Mark's for your coffee roaster, but there's no denying it looks great!

< 157 >

Cyberdeck

The plan behind Jason Benson's project was to build a working version of the "Cyberdeck" computers that feature in cyberpunk fiction, such as William Gibson's *Sprawl* novels, and the *Shadowrun* RPG universe.

STATS

BUILDER	Jason Benson
TIME TO BUILD	10 hours
COST TO BUILD	Approx. $100
DIFFICULTY LEVEL	Intermediate

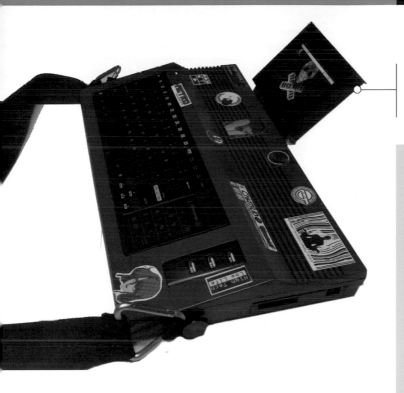

The display can slide inside the case so it can be carried around by its shoulder strap. It can also pivot to change its angle.

MATERIALS

- → Case from a Commodore 64
- → Raspberry Pi 3 (with case and fan)
- → Kmashi 10,000 mAh USB battery
- → Pazz wireless keyboard with trackpad
- → 4 port USB hub
- → HDMI splitter
- → HDMI to USB adaptor
- → USB to micro USB cable with a power switch
- → Styrene sheet plastic
- → Carriage bolts with inserts
- → Paint
- → Stickers
- → Sharp knife
- → Straight edge
- → Drill
- → Lighter or minitorch
- → Rotary tool
- → Glue

The Project

In the books and stories that inspired this project, a "Cyberdeck" is a portable computer that the user plugs into their brain using a neural connection. Obviously, Jason's creation doesn't have a neural interface, so he's substituted it with a set of video glasses.

The basis for the project's chassis was a broken Commodore 64 computer, which had the 1980s aesthetic that is common to the cyberpunk genre. However, Jason replaced the original keyboard and function keys with a wireless keyboard, trackpad, and USB hub.

//

The Code

This project is complex in terms of its physical fabrication, with some rather intricate wiring to put together and fit inside the case. However, as it runs on a stock install of Raspbian, there is no additional code.

//

< 159 >

The video cables take up
a lot of space inside the
case. It proved a challenge
to fit it all in, so careful
planning was needed.

Inside the vintage case is
a Raspberry Pi 3, powered
by a USB battery. The Pi
has several video options,
including a VGA port that can
plug into a monitor or video
glasses and an internal display
that can slide out and pivot
toward the user. Although this
slide-out display was hard to
build, Jason really wanted the
screen hidden when not in use,

so he fabricated a case for it
and built a sliding mechanism
from scratch.

This project required a lot of
customization and fabrication.
The display chassis and some
exterior covers were from a
styrene sheet, and a number
of holes had to be cut into the
Commodore's case. Finally,
to make it look more like a
machine that had seen some
use on the mean streets of a
cyberpunk city, Jason painted
it red, added a shoulder strap,
and had custom stickers
printed to badge it and add
some flavor.

How To Use This Idea

Jason's Cyberdeck can do anything a Pi-powered laptop
can do—the major difference is that you can retract the
Cyberdeck's screen and use video glasses for privacy.

< 160 >

The Builder

Before he moved into IT, Jason Benson (known online as "D10D3") was a clockmaker, professionally restoring antique clocks. This experience gave him a wide range of technical and fabrication skills, which he now applies to projects that fall somewhere between invention and art—fanciful designs that are as "real" and functional as possible.

Jason fell in love with the Raspberry Pi the first time he saw it. He knew he could build things with it that had always been out of reach before, such as wearable computers, robots, or computerized art. Jason's inspiration is quite unpredictable and he never knows what he'll be working on next. However, he tries to make sure he's always working on something!

TIPS

- Test fit all of your parts before you cut anything or glue them together.

- Always wear safety glasses and a mask when cutting or grinding with a rotary tool.

- Cut holes slightly smaller than you need and widen them with a hand file for a perfect fit. It's much easier to enlarge a hole than it is to make it smaller!

The style of the Cyberdeck was inspired by William Gibson's *Shadowrun* and *The Sprawl Trilogy* novels.

< 161 >

Tytelli Smartphone

While Apple and Samsung slug it out at the top of the global smartphone market, interesting Pi-based developments are happening in Tyler Spadgenske's workshop in Minnesota...

STATS

BUILDER	Tyler Spadgenske
TIME TO BUILD	30 hours
COST TO BUILD	Approx. $180
DIFFICULTY LEVEL	Intermediate

MATERIALS

→ Raspberry Pi 1 Model A+

→ Adafruit FONA uFL version cellular module

→ 3.5" touchscreen display

→ Camera module

→ Powerboost 500 basic boost convertor

→ GSM antenna

→ 1W 8 Ohm metal speaker

→ USB Wi-Fi adaptor

→ Electret microphone

→ 1200 mAh li-ion battery

→ 4-40 x ⅜" screws

→ M2.5 x 5mm screws

→ M2.5 x 20mm screws

→ M2 x 5mm screws

→ Slide switch

→ Wire

The Project

Tyler Spadgenske's Tytelli Smartphone is a remarkable project: it can make and receive calls, handle text messages, and even take pictures and upload them to online storage. Everything is enclosed in a 3D printed case and thanks to a 320 x 240 pixel touchscreen it all works without a physical keypad!

Although Tyler's Pi-powered smartphone isn't the first of its kind (Dave Hunt's PiPhone is widely accepted as the bearer of that honor), it certainly might be the most elaborate.

At its heart is a Raspberry Pi Model A+ coupled with a SIM800 cellular module (typically found on very old smartphones); a five-megapixel Raspberry Pi camera module; and a lithium-ion battery. Perhaps most impressive, though, is that the Tytelli runs its own custom software, written using Python.

///

The Code

All you need for the Tytelli is available via Tyler's online instructions (see page 219). The most important element is the custom operating system, "TYOS." This is a GUI overlay version of Raspbian (the project's true OS).

///

< 163 >

< 164 >

Making your own touchscreen display for a homemade smartphone may sound like an impossible task, but as Tyler's project proves, that's not the case.

How To Use This Idea

Like many other Tytelli builders, you might find a way to help Tyler improve his project if you build your own. Perhaps you can find a way to install your spin on a media player, for example, or even run a game of your own creation?

Tyler started thinking about making his own smartphone after reading the technical specifications of the original Raspberry Pi. He realized that it used a BCM2835 processor, which was commonly found in early smartphones. This gave him the idea to "turn the Pi back into a phone."

The project wasn't without its challenges, though. The hardest element of the construction was getting everything to work together. Getting the display to function was one thing, but connecting the cellular module, touchscreen, and camera—and then convincing them to function as a whole—presented a significant test.

Tyler rose to the challenge, though, resulting in a project that has been showered with praise and attention.

The Builder

Tyler Spadgenske came across the Raspberry Pi in 2013 and the following year he had his first starter kit. The home-schooled student from Buffalo, MN, set to work

teaching himself the Python programming language, and after a flurry of entry-level Pi electronics projects decided he was ready for something a little more ambitious.

In 2014—and still relatively new to the Raspberry Pi—he started work on a speech-controlled humanoid robot that he christened "Andy." The project was only a partial success, though, as Tyler struggled to get his creation to walk smoothly, and the speech synthesis was—in his own words—"mediocre."

Undeterred, he set out on another ambitious creation—to build a fully functioning smartphone. The result was the Tytelli, and this time around "mediocre" is definitely not an accurate description.

TIPS

- Assemble your smartphone a piece at a time. Connect the screen, and see if it works before you go further. Then connect the camera and test it before moving on. Don't solder everything all at once, as it just won't work.

- Develop a fundamental familiarity with the Raspberry Pi and electronics before you attempt to build your own Tytelli. It might be easier than you think to make a smartphone, but it's not the simplest project.

- Triple-check your electrical connections before applying power. Although the Pi itself is cheap, time isn't, so you don't want to be waiting for replacement parts.

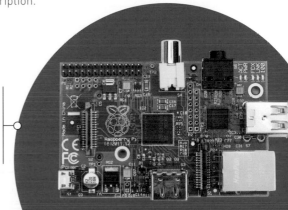

The inspiration for the project came when Tyler realized the Pi used a processor commonly found in early smartphones.

Media Center

1980s tech meets Raspberry Pi in this red retro refit, which is as happy streaming video as it is playing music.

STATS

BUILDER	Martin Mander
TIME TO BUILD	180 hours
COST TO BUILD	Approx. $120
DIFFICULTY LEVEL	Advanced

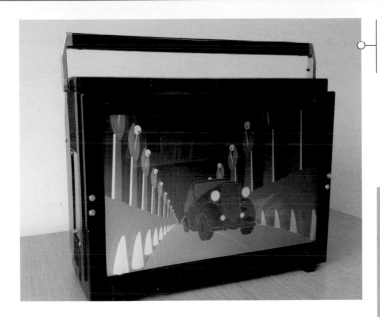

Martin originally intended to plug his media center into a TV, but realized the case was large enough to house its own screen.

MATERIALS

→ 1981 Sharp VC-2300H portable VCR
→ Raspberry Pi Model B+
→ USB hub
→ 4-way electrical socket
→ 4-way USB adaptor
→ Wireless adaptor
→ Microsoft USB IR receiver
→ USB mouse (dismantled)
→ 15" flat panel TV (dismantled)
→ Carbon Frog Arduino-based matrix clock
→ Electroluminescent wire
→ Gray spray primer
→ Red spray paint

The Project

Martin's Media Center is housed in a converted 1980s portable video recorder, which the builder picked up for under $10 on eBay. Initially he planned to just put a Raspberry Pi in it to connect to a regular TV, but soon realized that with its bulky internals removed there would be room for a whole lot more.

The VCR now has a Raspberry Pi Model B+ at its heart, with an Arduino-based clock and an electroluminescent wire "tape" that ejects to reveal the slots of a powered USB hub. Most importantly it also has an integrated 15-inch, flat-panel HD-screen at the back of the case, as well as a clear access panel at the side to show off the Raspberry Pi.

//

The Code

Martin's project uses the Raspbmc media center operating system, but this has now evolved into OSMC (Open Source Media Center). OSMC is a far superior operating system, which has a huge online following for mods and tweaks. It is also based on Debian Jessie, the same Linux version as Raspbian, so if you like to tinker under the hood the file structure will be very familiar. You can download OSMC at osmc.tv.

//

< 167 >

As well as electrical power, the Media Center uses removable batteries to power a custom eject mechanism and LEDs.

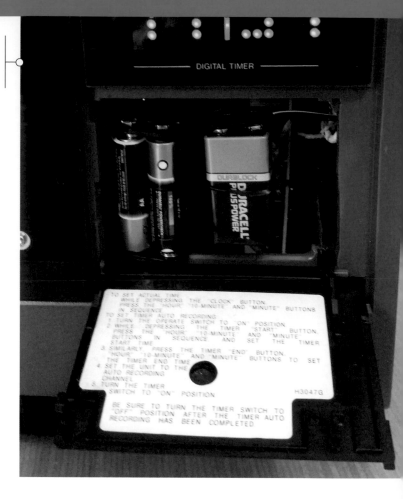

Although the VCR's original buttons are used for various functions, Martin spent a long time trying to get them to control the open-source Raspbmc software. In the end he used a dismantled mouse to handle the important button presses and left the rest to be controlled via a standard media center remote controller or mobile app.

Martin's Media Center currently does a great job of streaming video content via Wi-Fi, as well as playing Internet radio and various files from networked, USB, or internal storage devices. However, the standout feature for Martin is the color. He was all set to spray it black or brown, but changed his mind when his wife suggested going for "raspberry red." It was great advice and really gave the final product a lift.

Given its sophistication, it's perhaps surprising to discover that this was Martin's very

< 168 >

Utilizing old tech for your Pi projects is great, but you need to make sure you choose something that fits everything in!

Martin's build uses some of the VCR's original controls, which were made to work using the switches from a stripped-down USB mouse.

first Raspberry Pi project, so he was new to the world of GPIO and Python code. With his subsequent experience he knows he would now find it considerably easier to build, especially as the media center software has also evolved. With that in mind he vows to one day crack open the video recorder and commit to a proper rebuild!

How To Use This Idea

While you may have all kinds of ideas for things you can do with a Raspberry Pi, it won't hurt to finish your project in style with a nice outer casing. Using retro technology is a great starting point, and there's some beautiful old broken tech out there that's just begging to be repurposed (even if you just use the outer casing!). However, as Martin discovered, getting the original buttons to work can be a challenge.

< 169 >

The Builder

Martin Mander is passionate about the technology of his childhood. He has fond memories of his family's early video recorders and stereos, and enjoys turning classic pieces of tech into new, functional items using modern components. It was after he had converted several retro televisions to LCD screens that he was introduced to Raspberry Pi. Martin looked into the technology and was immediately struck by the Raspberry Pi's capability and size: the old tech he loves is naturally huge, while the Raspberry Pi is tiny, making it ideal to fit inside.

The media center was a real labor of love for Martin and although it turned out exactly as he'd hoped, he resolved to make future projects more straightforward. He has since built a retro-style Internet radio (which you can see on pages 148–151) and is working on a variety of Internet of Things projects, using the Pi to harness the power of Amazon's *Alexa* voice service.

A clear acrylic window reveals the media center's beating heart—a Raspberry Pi Model B+.

< 170 >

TIPS

● When you're building a project using published software or code, keep a lookout for new versions and releases that fix problems or unlock new functions.

● Community maker events are fantastic places to get inspiration and discover new add-ons and accessories. For example, Martin found out about the Carbon Frog clock at a maker fair—he would not have known it existed otherwise.

● Don't forget to check your local dollar store for potential project components. This type of retailer often stocks items containing useful LEDs, switches, and sensors that can be stripped out and reused in your builds.

Martin's project is the perfect blend of old and new, with classic form meeting modern function.

< 171 >

Build it! ➡ Lunchbox Laptop

This easy-to-make portable computer has many of the capabilities of a regular laptop, but it is much cheaper to build and far more fun to carry around.

STATS

BUILDER	Jason Benson
TIME TO BUILD	2 hours
COST TO BUILD	Approx. $125
DIFFICULTY LEVEL	Beginner

MATERIALS

→ Lunchbox
→ Small 12V composite LCD
→ Micro USB Cable
→ 2.1mm male 12V plug
→ 2 x 9V battery connectors
→ 2 x 9V batteries
→ Raspberry Pi 1 or Pi 2/3 with an RCA adaptor for headphone socket
→ Case for Raspberry Pi
→ Short male-to-male RCA cable (or male-to-male adaptor)
→ DC 12V to 5V USB power convertor
→ 2.1mm (1) female to (2) male "Y" cable
→ Small wireless keyboard

The Project

The Lunchbox Laptop is a Pi-powered computer built into a regular lunchbox. With Wi-Fi, web browsing, and word processing at your fingertips, it's a practical project and also a guaranteed talking point: open it at a coffee shop or restaurant and people are guaranteed to come over and ask questions!

The project started when Jason bought a small lunchbox in a sale. He didn't know what he would use it for, but liked the look and size of it. Weeks later, while he was trying to figure out an unrelated problem, he glanced up and realized he had everything he needed to build a lunchbox laptop sitting in his workshop. Gripped by inspiration, he threw the first version together in an hour!

The Builder

Jason Benson is an IT professional from Philadelphia, PA. He is a maker, hardware and software hacker, artist, and dreamer with an insatiable need to build things and modify them. Put simply, he describes himself as a "geeky jack-of-all-trades."

Jason grew up using 8-bit computers in the 1980s. While he's closely followed the rapid development of computers and loves modern fast machines, part of him fondly recalls the simple, easy to understand machines of his youth. So when he heard about an affordable little computer that could fit anywhere—the Raspberry Pi—he knew he wanted to make things with it.

Get the code
magpi.cc/easy-raspberry-pi

TUTORIAL

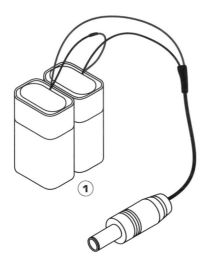

1. Make A Battery Pack

To power the project you need to make an 18V battery pack using two 9V batteries wired in series. Start by sliding a small piece of shrink tube over the negative (black) wire from one of your 9V battery connectors. Solder the black wire to the positive (red) wire from the other battery connector and seal the connection with the shrink tube.

Solder the remaining positive and negative wires to the corresponding wires of a 2.1mm male plug, again sealing each connection with shrink tube to prevent shorts.

Finally, plug your 9V batteries into the connectors and you have an 18V battery with an easy-to-use plug.

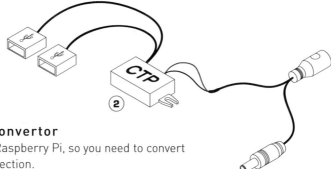

2. Attach The Power Convertor

18V is too much power for a Raspberry Pi, so you need to convert it to a 5V and add a USB connection.

To do this, take the 2.1mm female-to-male Y cable and cut off one of the two male ends. Strip the end to reveal the positive and negative wires and solder these to the corresponding wires on the power convertor (remember to seal all of your connections with shrink tube).

Now, when you plug your battery into the Y cable, the power will go to both the power convertor and the other male plug (which will go to the LCD).

< 174 >

3. Bench Test

Using a micro USB cable, connect one of the power convertor's USB sockets to the Raspberry Pi's power socket.

With an RCA cable (or male-to-male adaptor), plug the yellow video plug from the LCD into the yellow RCA jack on the Raspberry Pi.

Connect the male plug from the 2.1mm Y cable to the red power jack on the LCD.

Finally, connect the battery pack to the 2.1mm Y cable. The Raspberry Pi should start up automatically and after a few seconds the display should light up and show it booting.

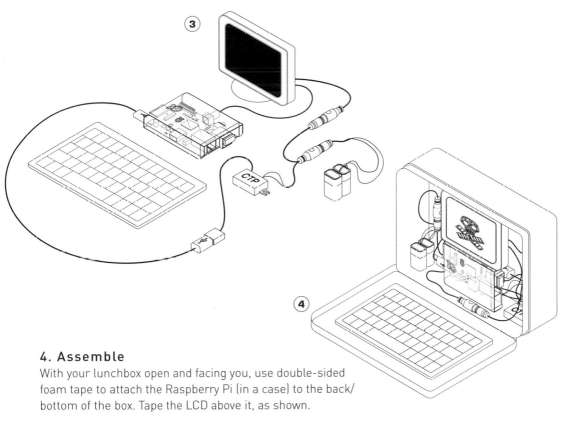

4. Assemble

With your lunchbox open and facing you, use double-sided foam tape to attach the Raspberry Pi (in a case) to the back/bottom of the box. Tape the LCD above it, as shown.

Using more foam tape, attach a Velcro strap at the lower left and use that to hold the batteries in. You should also use foam tape to fit the power convertor at the right side of the lunchbox.

Finish up by taping the keyboard to the inside of the lunchbox's lid. Remember that if you need to get to the back of the keyboard to replace its batteries or charge it, it may be best to tape along one edge so the keyboard can hinge upward.

< 175 >

Build it!

Yogurt Maker

Although you can buy specialist yogurt-making machines, they were all too small for Sebastian Schneckener's family, who consume more than one gallon of yogurt each week!

STATS

BUILDER	Sebastian Schneckener
TIME TO BUILD	20 hours
COST TO BUILD	Approx. $95
DIFFICULTY LEVEL	Intermediate

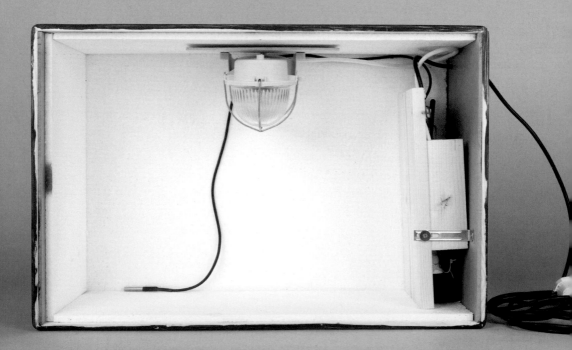

MATERIALS

→ Raspberry Pi (any model)
→ 25W tungsten light bulb (not energy saving)
→ Solid state relay
→ Thermo sensor type DS18B20
→ 3 x 500 Ohm resistors (for the SSR and LEDs)
→ 4.7K Ohm resistor (for the thermo sensor)
→ Green, red, and yellow LEDs
→ Transistor 2N3904
→ 3ft cable suitable for high-voltage wiring
→ Short pieces of cable for low-voltage wiring
→ 5V power source
→ An enclosure (a wooden box, as used here, is ideal)
→ Polystyrene sheeting to line enclosure (approx. ½" thick)
→ Wood/plastic glue
→ Drill
→ Cutters
→ Screwdriver
→ Pliers
→ Soldering iron

The Project

The science behind making yogurt is very straightforward. The whole process can be done in the kitchen except for one vital step: the yogurt culture needs to be at a constant temperature of 100°F for more than five hours.

At a basic level, this yogurt-making machine is simply an enclosure with a temperature sensor and a heating device. A Raspberry Pi monitors and regulates the temperature, maintaining the necessary 100°F while the yogurt culture grows. It also logs the process and provides some diagnostic LEDs. The end result? Plenty of delicious homemade yogurt!

The Builder

For Sebastian Schneckener, the Raspberry Pi is a cheap resource to tinker with. He's used his Raspberry Pi for many different projects, such as a Time Machine backup device for his Apple Mac computer and as a music server. However, it was not until he put it into a yogurt maker that it started to fulfill a very real need for himself and his family.

Get the code
quartoknows.com/page/raspberry-pi

< 177 >

TUTORIAL

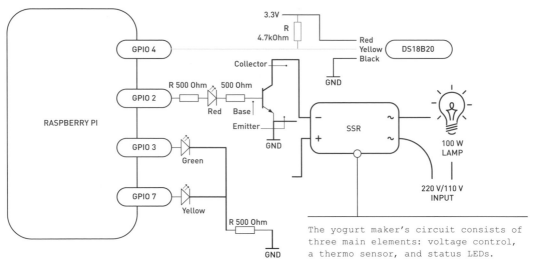

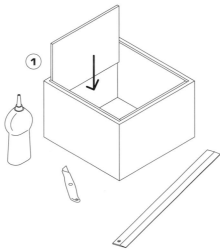

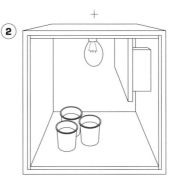

The yogurt maker's circuit consists of three main elements: voltage control, a thermo sensor, and status LEDs.

1. Build Your Enclosure

You can build any enclosure you like, but it needs to be insulated with polystyrene. The prototype for this project was simply a large, polystyrene box, which was both enclosure and insulator. However, this version is made of wood with polystyrene sheets cut to size and glued into the box to insulate it.

2. Add A Lamp

The heat source is a regular light bulb mounted inside the box (it's important that this is a tungsten/halogen bulb that runs at a warm temperature). A low-wattage bulb in the region of 25W is perfect for this project, as more powerful bulbs can run too hot. Make a hole in the side of your enclosure for the lamp's power supply cable to pass through.

< 178 >

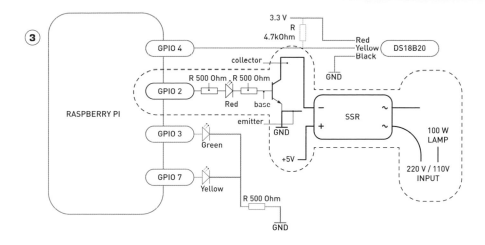

3. Wire Up The Voltage Control

The project requires the lamp to be turned on and off to maintain a constant temperature of 100°F inside the box. However, a 25W lamp cannot be switched on directly by the 3.3V output of a Raspberry Pi, so we're using a solid state relay (SSR). As the SSR requires 5V, and the Pi delivers 3.3V, an additional transistor is used to "amplify" the power from the GPIO. As this stage is dealing with high-voltage current (220V/110V for the lamp), have someone check over your wiring if you are in any way unsure about what you are doing.

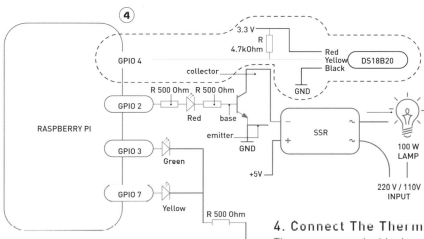

4. Connect The Thermo Sensor

The temperature inside the yogurt maker is measured using a thermo sensor, which is connected to a 3.3V feed, ground, and a GPIO pin on the Raspberry Pi, as shown here.

< 179 >

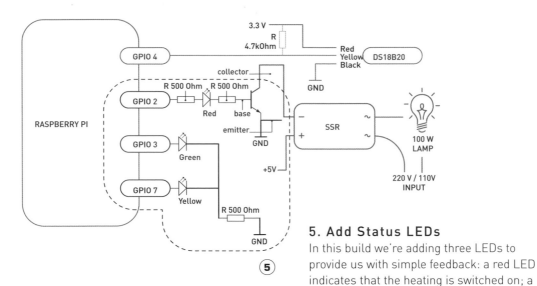

3.3 V

R
4.7kOhm

GPIO 4

Red
Yellow — DS18B20
Black

GND

collector

R 500 Ohm · R 500 Ohm

GPIO 2

Red   base

emitter

GND

SSR

~
~

+

100 W
LAMP

220 V / 110V
INPUT

RASPBERRY PI

GPIO 3

Green

+5V

GPIO 7

Yellow

R 500 Ohm

GND

(5)

5. Add Status LEDs

In this build we're adding three LEDs to provide us with simple feedback: a red LED indicates that the heating is switched on; a green LED shows that the temperature is within the correct range; and a yellow LED indicates the temperature is too high. In total, ten parts need to be soldered on the breakout board.

6. Sensor Support

You need to add support for the thermo sensor by adding the following line to */boot/config.txt*. You can edit this file with Nano by running **sudo nano /boot/config.txt**. Once the file is open, scroll to the bottom and type the following code:

dtoverlay=w1-gpio

Reboot your Pi using **sudo reboot** and open Nano. Copy the code *thermostat.py* and *readTemperature.py* from the book's website and save them to your Pi.

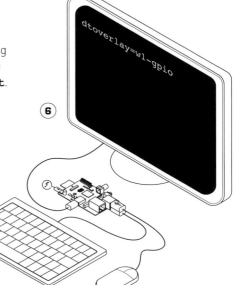

(6)

< 180 >

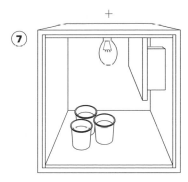

7. Running Your Yogurt Maker

The main Python script used to control the temperature in the box is *thermostat.py*, which is pre-installed with Python in the Raspbian operating system. *thermostat.py* can be provided with a single target temperature, or upper and lower temperature limits.

Every ten seconds, *thermostat. py* will check the temperature in the enclosure, and use the information to switch the SSR on or off (to activate the lamp) and control the diagnostic LEDs. It also writes the status to a log file, which is saved automatically as *thermostat.txt*.

After assembling your yogurt maker, start up **sudo python3 thermostat. py**. The red LED should light up to indicate the heating circuit is functioning, and the lamp should come on to start heating your box. After a couple of minutes, the temperature inside the box will have reached 100°F, where it will be maintained while you make your yogurt.

TIPS

- You can find out more about using the DS18B20 thermo sensor at learn.adafruit.com/adafruits-raspberry-pi-lesson-11-ds18b20-temperature-sensing/overview.

- It's a good idea to build the circuit on a breadboard and test it before soldering everything together. There's nothing particularly difficult about the circuitry for this project, but it's worth checking everything works before you commit to the design.

- As well as cow's milk, you could also try using alternatives such as goat, yak, or even camel milk! You can make Greek yogurt by filtering it through a cloth, and on hot days you could make yourself a refreshing Turkish ayran by combining yogurt, water, and salt.

Make Some Yogurt!

Contrary to some claims, when it comes to making yogurt it isn't necessary to sterilize your equipment—your yogurt culture is going to outcompete anything else.

Start the yogurt maker heating up, as outlined in the previous step. While this is happening, heat some milk on a stove until it starts simmering (it should be at least 160°F). This is required for denaturing milk proteins. Put the milk pan in a sink or bowl filled with cold water to cool it quickly down to just above 105°F.

Mix your milk with a glass of regular yogurt—this will add the valuable yogurt cultures (bacteria from the genus *Lactobacillus*). Stir well and partition the milk into containers of a suitable size before putting them into the yogurt maker.

After five hours you can take out the containers, which will now contain your yogurt. However, it is best to let it cool in the fridge before eating— warm yogurt doesn't taste particularly nice!

< 181 >

6

ART PI

Where science meets art

The Internet Of LEGO®

Cory Guynn's "living" LEGO city demonstrates what is possible using the Internet of Things, giving us an insight into how our urban environments might function in the future.

STATS

BUILDER	Cory Guynn
TIME TO BUILD	1½ years
COST TO BUILD	Approx. $2000 (mostly on LEGO)
DIFFICULTY LEVEL	Intermediate–Advanced

MATERIALS

→ 2 x Raspberry Pi
→ BeagleBone Green
→ 2 x Arduino Uno
→ 1 x Arduino Mega
→ 2 x Arduino Nano
→ 2 x Cactus Micro (Arduino Lilypad clones with ESP8266)
→ 5 x WeMos ESP8266 dev boards
→ 2 x NodeMCU ESP8266 dev boards
→ 1 x WioLink ESP8266 dev board
→ Ubuntu desktop
→ Ubuntu AWS hosted server

INPUT SENSORS:

→ Ultrasonic proximity
→ Infrared
→ Reed
→ RFID
→ Motion
→ Photo-resistors

OUTPUTS

→ Motors & servos
→ LEDs & addressable LED strips
→ OLED screens
→ 8 x 8 LED matrix
→ Cisco Meraki CMX & CxCap API
→ Transport for London API
→ Weather API
→ Google Maps API
→ ThingSpeak charting

< 185 >

The Project

When Cory heard that the Internet of Things would become a $14 trillion business within a few years, he wanted to understand what technologies were driving that business; what the software, hardware, communication, and use cases were that would help form this industry. However, as a pre-sales systems engineer, he often found himself talking about solutions and ideas struggling to demonstrate concepts, so he decided that he would not only explore the technology behind the IoT, but create a "proof of concept" by building a living city out of LEGO®.

The resulting Internet of LEGO contains a number of sub-projects, all connected and linked through the Internet. Although there are too many individual items to list, highlights include a LEGO train schedule that uses the Transport for London API, Node-RED, and an OLED display on a Raspberry Pi. The trains are infrared controlled, using proximity sensors and a transceiver to automate them with a Raspberry Pi, and also Wi-Fi controlled via a NodeMCU ESP8266 module and motor driver.

///

The Code

The Internet of LEGO's code works by sending information through a network to achieve a task. This is similar to how a Twitter message gets entered in your phone, goes to a server, and then is sent back out to your followers.

///

All of the LEGO city's functions are controlled by information terminals that receive data from the Internet.

< 186 >

The trains use real-time London transport data to set their schedules!

TIPS

- The Raspberry Pi and Arduino are perfect complements to one another. The Raspberry Pi is excellent for high-level coding and general computing, while Arduino and ESP8266 microcontrollers are great for repetitive or time-sensitive GPIO functions.

- You may prefer to code in higher-level languages, such as JavaScript or Python (rather than lower-level languages like C/C++). If this is the case, you'll spend more time on the Raspberry Pi, using Node-RED or JavaScript.

There is also a LEGO weather station that uses a Cactus Micro (Arduino/ESP8266), DHT-11 weather sensor, photo sensor, and MQTT messaging system to generate data charts via Google Charts and ThingSpeak; energy saving city lights that contain motion sensors, with a timeout that saves electricity and communicates motion in a room; and a LEGO elevator that uses an ultrasonic proximity sensor and motor (again via the Raspberry Pi).

Node-RED and JohnnyFive are used to manipulate the various systems directly or logically

attached to the system. It was the JohnnyFive.io JavaScript framework for robotics that got Cory really interested in translating web technology into the physical space. It became really fun to control lights, servos, and sensors using a familiar web language, and by attaching an Arduino Mega to a Raspberry Pi via

How To Use This Idea

The easiest way to begin a similar project is to get a Raspberry Pi and have a play with Node-RED. Then get a Grove starter kit that allows you to easily connect sensors, motors, and displays. Start by creating a small building and introducing a lighting system, then build up your city over time.

< 187 >

USB he instantly had control over several GPIOs to control all aspects of the Internet of LEGO® city.

Cory then discovered the power of Node-RED. This IBM project, which acts as visual plumbing for the Internet of Things, provided a clever and powerful way to connect multiple systems and provide analytics or trigger workflows.

Much of what Cory is building is pioneering, which means he finds himself inventing or innovating on a regular basis. However, this is precisely what makes this ongoing project so incredibly rewarding. Because he has been able to overcome these challenges, Cory is making a real impact on the Internet of Things and the maker community.

Hidden under the city are the electronic components that control every function. They are carefully labeled and laid out so they can be changed and adapted for new buildings and objects.

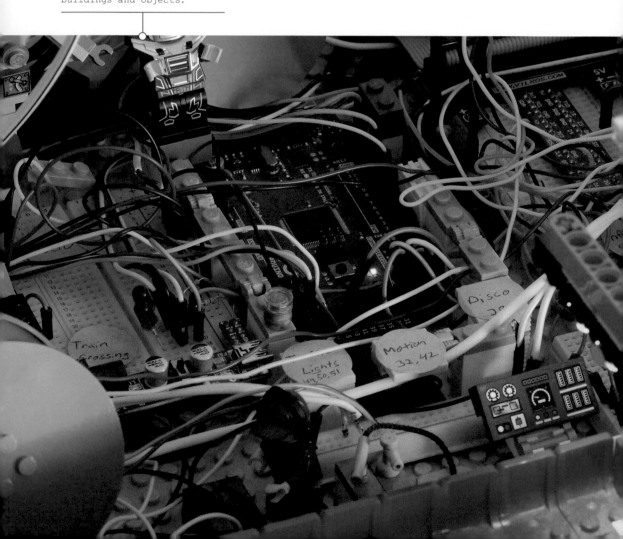

The Builder

Cory Guynn is a 35-year-old systems engineer at Cisco Meraki who loves the evolution of technology, cloud network solutions, and the study of the Internet of Things. The Raspberry Pi has been a major inspiration for Cory because of its ability to run a full Linux operating system on a credit card-sized computer; he sees the potential for many Internet of Things services to be orchestrated on this affordable, compact, and flexible system.

Cory's Internet of LEGO project has garnered a lot of attention, not only featuring in many magazines, but also winning the Internet of Things of the Year Award, 2016. Another major positive from Cory's perspective is that building with Raspberry Pi has given him the chance to use skills he learned at school, but doesn't need in his regular work: in building his city he has been able to practice various programming languages, design multiple electrical circuits, and, of course, buy a bunch of LEGO!

The city's lights are time sensitive, so the little LEGO people can have a night life!

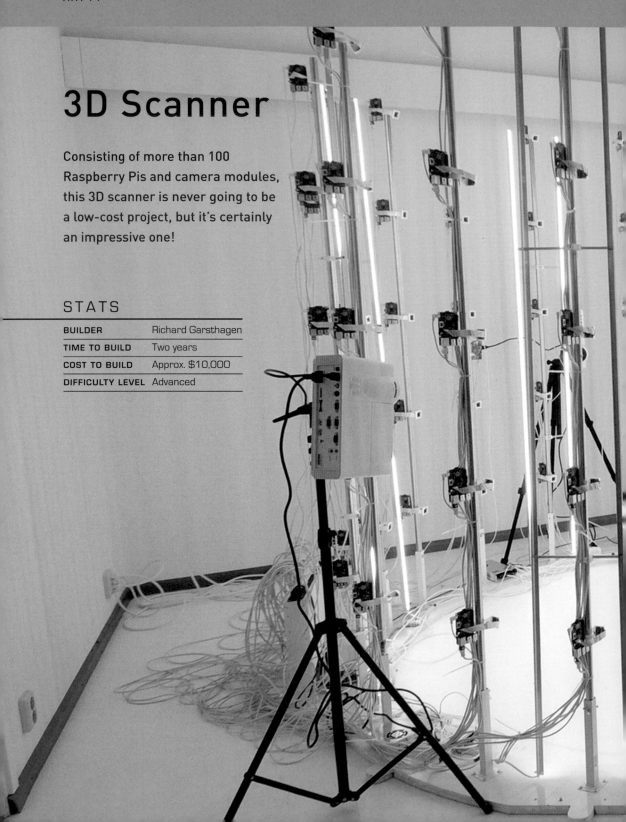

3D Scanner

Consisting of more than 100 Raspberry Pis and camera modules, this 3D scanner is never going to be a low-cost project, but it's certainly an impressive one!

STATS

BUILDER	Richard Garsthagen
TIME TO BUILD	Two years
COST TO BUILD	Approx. $10,000
DIFFICULTY LEVEL	Advanced

MATERIALS

→ 100+ Raspberry Pis

→ 100+ Pi camera modules

→ Ethernet cables & network switches

→ 5V 60 Amp power supplies

→ Metal poles

→ Plastic 3D-printed brackets

→ High-power LED strips

→ 24V power supplies for LEDs

→ Projectors with Raspberry Pi units attached via HDMI

The Project

Richard Garsthagen's 3D Scanner calls upon a network of over 100 Raspberry Pis with camera modules attached, which can all take a picture at the exact same moment. The Raspberry Pis and camera modules are mounted in a large, "full body" scanner constructed using simple poles (radiator pipes bought from a DIY store) and self-designed, 3D-printed brackets. Additional Raspberry Pi units are used to add noise projection using computer projectors, with further units controlling all the LED lights.

< 193 >

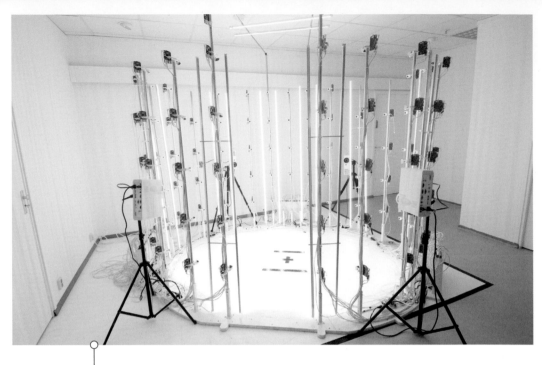

The 3D scanner creates a ring of cameras around the subject to ensure it is recorded from every angle.

The resulting "scanner" is capable of creating more than 200 images simultaneously, which can be used in conjunction with photogrammetry software to create digital 3D models of people, animals, or anything else that is placed within the "scanning circle." This model can then be printed in miniature, in full color, using a 3D powder printer.

Of course, 3D scanning with multiple cameras isn't new. However, it is traditionally done with regular digital SLR cameras. At over $500 each, that would mean a design like this would cost in excess of $50,000. By using low-cost Raspberry Pi units and camera modules instead, Richard's scanner cost around $10,000— a significant cost reduction.

//

The Code

The code for Richard's 3D Scanner is written in Python. Most code uses the IP protocol to talk to other computers, but if you want to be able to talk to multiple computers at once you can use the UDP protocol, which supports Multicasting (shouting out a single network packet to multiple machines). Sending UDP traffic is fairly easy in most programming languages, including Python.

//

< 194 >

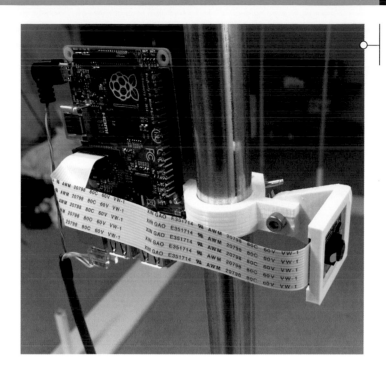

Each Raspberry Pi and camera module is attached to the scanner's frame using a 3D-printed bracket.

Richard's project has many technological facets, including special multicast network programming; electronics to control multiple powerful LED strips, graphics, and computer projectors to display extra noise projection; and 3D-printed brackets that attach each Raspberry Pi and camera module to the frame.

After initial testing, Richard took the scanner to a Dutch Maker Faire, where he offered everyone a free 3D scan of themselves. The reaction was amazing, as the scanner is very big and has a distinct "sci-fi" feel to it. People didn't understand why he was offering his scans for free, but the simple reason is that

Richard loves being able to make people happy with mini figures of their kids, animals, or themselves. As an extension of this he has made miniature figures of a number of terminally ill people and older animals in the past two years, creating a lasting memory for their families and partners.

The project was—and still is— a learning journey for Richard, who is continuing to develop

and improve the 3D scanner. In 2014 he decided to publish the project online, although he didn't think anyone else would build a 3D scanner themselves. However, there are now over 100 replicas around the world—which accounts for more than 10,000 Raspberry Pis!

How To Use This Idea

To scan people (or any other subject that might move) it is best to use multiple cameras. However, it is possible to make a 3D scanner with just one Raspberry Pi and camera, a laser line, and a turntable. The most well known setup is the FabScan Pi kit, which is available online for less than $200.

< 195 >

Using Raspberry Pis meant Richard's scanner cost him around $10,000. That's not cheap, but if he'd used digital SLR cameras it would likely have cost him $50,000+.

The 3D scans produce digital 3D models that can be printed using a 3D printer.

The Builder

Richard Garsthagen is from Zoetermeer in the Netherlands. He started playing with Arduino around 2010, and two years later began to experiment with Raspberry Pi. He always has multiple projects on the go, and depending on the type of project will base it on either Arduino or Raspberry Pi.

In the past years Richard has made a number of projects, including simple robots, an automatic Nerf gun target-shooting range, electronic puzzles, split-flap display systems, a race lap timer, a photo booth that posts images automatically to Facebook, and more besides!

< 196 >

TIPS

● In the beginning, don't overthink things or make them overly complex. Instead, start small and grow your idea.

● Before you start, see if someone else has done something similar. If they have, you can learn from his or her experience and maybe adjust your design accordingly.

● Never worry about whether you can finish a project or not—It's about the journey, not the destination! You may start projects that you don't finish, but the knowledge and experience you gain along the way will help with other projects in the future.

As well as printing mini statues with a 3D printer, the files created by Richard's scanner can be output using a CNC machine. The model is "sliced up" and each slice is cut out from wood. The slices are then glued on top of each other to create a statue.

< 197 >

BeetBox

The BeetBox is beautifully simple and surreal: just tap a beet to play a beat!

The BeetBox proves your Raspberry Pi projects don't have to be too serious. In fact, the more fun they are, the more you might learn.

STATS

BUILDER	Scott Garner
TIME TO BUILD	Approx. 80 hours
COST TO BUILD	$100
DIFFICULTY LEVEL	Advanced

MATERIALS

→ Raspberry Pi

→ MPR121 capacitive touch sensor

→ LM386-based amplifier

→ Timber & woodworking tools (for enclosure)

→ Beets

The Project

Scott Garner's work is typically intelligent and well considered, and that is certainly true of his BeetBox. The project is also unashamedly playful, which becomes immediately obvious when you appreciate the pun in its name.

Encapsulating the concept of "invisible technology," BeetBox does not look especially technical at first glance; six beets sit on an understated wooden rack, and that's it. At least that's it until a curious observer touches one of the vegetables and a drum beat or other sound rings out from the hidden speaker!

///

The Code

A Python script is available from Scott (details on page 219), which lets contact with the beets trigger particular sounds. The code that interfaces with the MPR121 capacitive touch sensor builds on an Arduino example by Jim Lindblom.

///

< 199 >

How To Use This Idea

There aren't too many practical applications for the BeetBox, unless you count its potential as a captivating party centerpiece. However, it does provide plenty of inspiration for what is possible with "invisible technology." Constructing something similar won't only teach you how to disguise technology, but you might pick up some carpentry skills as well.

One "component" that won't last long is the beets. Fortunately, they are significantly cheaper than most musical hardware!

<200>

Under the modest wooden shell lurks a fairly intricate electronics project, even though it uses just a few components. The biggest challenge was to get an MPR121 capacitive touch sensor to "talk" to the Pi. To achieve this, Scott ported over some existing code for that particular chip, and followed some online pointers to get things to work fluidly. After that, he wrote a bespoke Python script that would trigger the sounds.

Ultimately, the effort was well worth it and seeing tentative BeetBox first-timers try the instrument is delightful: the project inspires trepidation, laughter, and satisfaction in all who meet it.

The Builder

Scott Garner is a long-time devotee to creative projects using the Arduino single-board microcontrollers. When Raspberry Pi arrived he was drawn to the additional power and flexibility the newcomer offered—both in isolation and when coupled with an Arduino.

The builder has also developed a fascination with what he terms "invisible technology," where electronic components are obscured within more traditional objects that do not immediately suggest contemporary gadgetry.

His interactive work *Still Life*, for example, presented what appeared to be an ordinary painting hung on a gallery wall. The painting was, however, an interactive 3D scene, with motion sensors hidden within its frame. As a result, when *Still Life* was tilted, the "painted" objects in the scene would react accordingly, tumbling from their positions as the frame moved.

TIPS

● The easiest way to get started with touch-based projects is to pick up a Makey Makey board, which transforms almost anything you choose into a touchable input device.

● Although Scott constructed an audio amp from scratch using salvaged parts, it is also possible to plug the Pi directly into an external speaker or headphones.

● Remember that you're not limited to screens and buttons when coming up with ways to interact with technology. There are a lot of amazing sensors and actuators out there that are well documented and fairly easy to use, so try to come up with something new.

< 201 >

Erica The Cyber Rhino

Erica The Cyber Rhino demonstrates that with a little thought a Raspberry Pi can be the perfect engine for positive change.

This rhino is a work of art.
Please do not climb on it as this could result in injury.

MATERIALS

Erica contains hundreds of parts, but some of the most important are:

→ 5 x Raspberry Pis

→ 2 x cameras & servos

→ Amplifier & speaker

→ 2 x Android-based tablet computers

→ Fiberglass rhino shell

STATS

BUILDER	Various
TIME TO BUILD	800 hours (including design)
COST TO BUILD	Approx. $5000 (including $2500 for the rhino shell)
DIFFICULTY LEVEL	Advanced

Webcam eyes give Erica the ability to "see" the crowds she often attracts, as well as read QR codes.

The Project

Erica is many things. She is a fiberglass sculpture, certainly, but more than that she is a means to raise awareness about rhino conservation, and a physical hub to bring together many interactive and intersecting technologies.

The concept for Erica came about when Marwell Zoo contacted a group within the University of Southampton, UK. The zoological park was promoting rhino conservation by placing a series of artworks in the local area and wanted to invite the University to contribute to the project.

//

The Code

A great deal of the code used for Erica's various systems of interaction is available at the rhino's devoted website (ericatherhino.org). You may not need every element for your own Raspberry Pi sculpture, but the separate pieces of code are remarkably useful and informative.

//

The University team didn't hesitate to sign up, but it wanted to do more than simply give a rhino-shaped fiberglass shell an eye-catching exterior. Instead, the team wanted to pack its rhino with electronic

<203>

components and deliver a truly interactive artwork—and that's exactly what it did.

The result is Erica The Cyber Rhino, who sports an impressive function list. She has webcams for eyes, allowing her to read QR codes and "see" the crowds she attracts; she features a speaker to give her a voice; independently controllable RGB and regular LEDs; touch sensors; and interactive touchscreens. Together, these technologies enable Erica to provide a local Wi-Fi network, interact with the smartphones of passersby, read relevant Tweets, and unleash authentic rhino sounds. Her moving ears give her a little character and life, and, of course, she sports a cyber-themed paint job. And the powerhouse behind all these abilities? Five regular Raspberry Pis.

A closer look at Erica The Cyber Rhino reveals that the sculpture is packed with interactive technology.

<204>

Erica sports her own custom circuitry, emblazoned with a rhino silhouette, which shows just how much detail went into the project.

While Erica is now retired and displayed in the relative tranquility of the foyer at the University of Southampton's Mountbatten Building, she used to stand in a busy shopping mall, where she would frequently attract curious youngsters. That meant that she not only needed to be technologically and physically robust, but safe for those wishing to explore her interactions and perhaps get a little too close.

Thanks to some thoughtful design, she passed each of those tests capably, but it was the Raspberry Pi assigned as her "brain" that really set her apart. A single Raspberry Pi processed the inputs from Erica's various sensors, and generated the appropriate outputs, such as moving her eyes or ears, or activating lights and sounds.

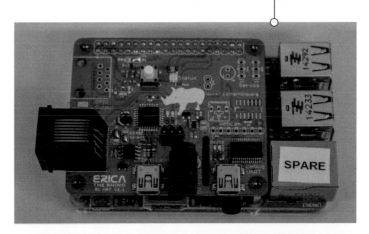

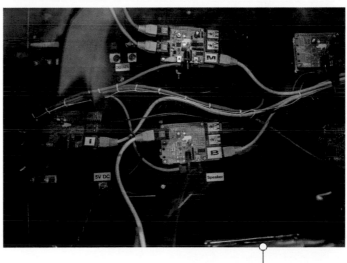

A total of five Raspberry Pis power Erica's diverse range of functions.

<205>

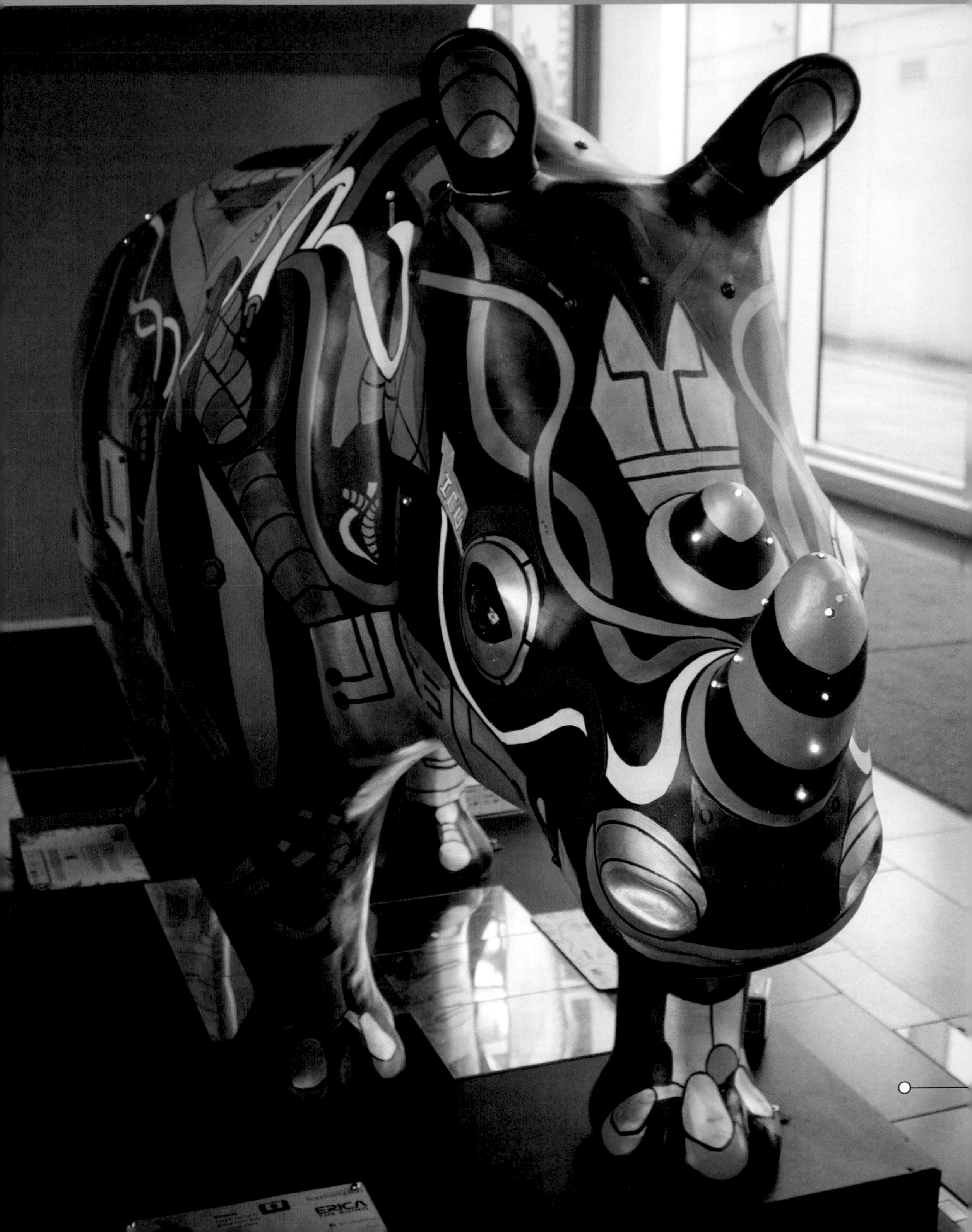

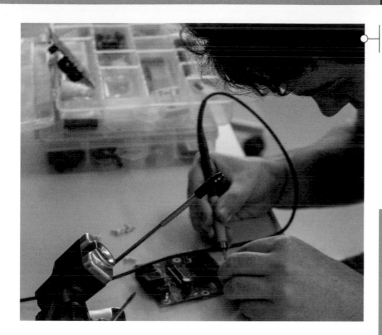

A wide range of skills and specialties were required to bring Erica to life.

The Builders

The team behind Erica The Cyber Rhino consisted mainly of staff and students from the Electronics and Computer Science department at the highly regarded University of Southampton, UK.

However, making Erica a reality took more than coding and computational engineering, with several other people from around the university campus brought on board to assist: Erica needed support from individuals with management skills, help from an IT team, and the services

of a handful of traditional artists to give her an attention-grabbing look.

The result was a core team with an impressive mix of skills, bringing together a range of practical, creative, and technological insights. That diversity is a key part of the reason why the interactive rhino sculpture has enjoyed so much success, and proves the power of collaboration in making projects that thrive.

It's not just the technology that sets Erica The Cyber Rhino apart from its peers; it was just as important to get the cyber-themed paintwork right as well.

How To Use This Idea

Making a full-sized fiberglass rhino sculpture is likely beyond the means of most Raspberry Pi owners, but you can still take inspiration from this project. Take a closer look at Erica's inner workings and you'll find myriad ideas that can be incorporated into your own Pi-powered artwork, which could perhaps be housed in a teddy bear or a hollow toy.

<207>

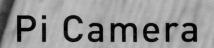

Pi Camera

A lot of Raspberry Pi projects utilize a camera module. This starter project will show you how you can connect a camera, enabling your Pi to start shooting video or stills.

STATS

BUILDER	Henry Budden
TIME TO BUILD	Under one hour
COST TO BUILD	Approx. $25
DIFFICULTY LEVEL	Beginner

MATERIALS

→ Raspberry Pi
→ Raspberry Pi camera module (with ribbon cable)
→ Keyboard
→ Case (optional)

The Project

A Pi Camera can be built during a lunch break, and all you need to get it up and running is a Raspberry Pi and a camera module. With a few simple additions you could then turn it into a spy camera, a wildlife trap camera, a stop-motion animation rig, or even your own security station.

However, before you get to that, knowing how to connect the camera, set up the software, and capture images is essential. Fortunately, this is all as easy as it is important, so even if this is your first Raspberry Pi project it is well within your reach!

The Builder

Technology has fascinated Henry his entire life, and he was lucky enough to be one of the first people to get his hands on a Raspberry Pi when it launched in 2012.

Since then he's been making his own Raspberry Pi projects, although he admits he sometimes breaks things as much as he makes them. That's all part of learning how to build great projects, though!

TIPS

● The official Raspberry Pi camera module is the perfect choice for this project, and many more projects besides.

● You can build on this project by making a stand to hold the camera upright.

Get the code

quartoknows.com/page/raspberry-pi

<209>

1. Ground Yourself

When your Raspberry Pi camera module arrives it will be protected by a special anti-static bag. When you unpack it, there's a small chance that the static carried in your body could damage the new camera module, so ground yourself by touching a radiator or metal computer casing first.

2. Connect The Camera

Connect the long, flat ribbon cable running from the camera module to your Raspberry Pi; you should find the right socket between your Pi's HDMI and Ethernet connectors. Make sure that the shiny connectors on the ribbon cable are facing toward the HDMI socket.

Secure the ribbon cable firmly in place, by pulling up the piece of black plastic on the connector, inserting the cable, and then pressing the plastic back down again. The cable should be locked in nice and snug.

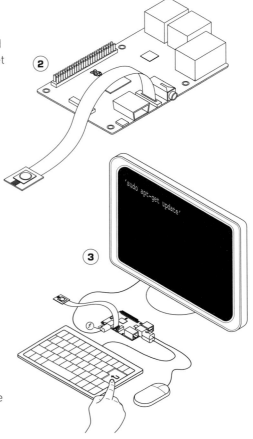

3. Activate The Camera

Open your Raspberry Pi's terminal and type:

```
sudo apt-get update
```

Press *Enter*, and then type:

```
sudo apt-get upgrade
```

Press *Enter* again.

Select *Preferences* from the dropdown menu at the top left corner of the screen, and then *Raspberry Pi Configuration*. From the window that opens select the *Interfaces* tab and check that the *Camera* setting is enabled before clicking *OK*.

< 210 >

4. Reboot Your Pi

If you have to make a change to the settings, you'll need to reboot your Raspberry Pi. Once your Pi has rebooted (or if you didn't need to change anything at step 3) open LXTerminal to start shooting photographs or video.

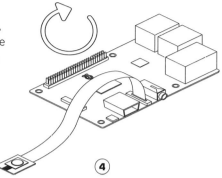

5. Shoot A Still Image

If you want to take a still image, aim the camera at your subject and type the following into LXTerminal, replacing ***** with the filename you want to give the image:

```
raspistill -o *****.jpeg
```

Press *Enter* and a short preview will appear on screen, before the camera takes a shot. The image will be saved in your Raspberry Pi's home directory (by default this will be named "Pi" unless you change it).

6. Shoot Video

To record a short video, type the following into LXTerminal.

```
raspivid -o *****.h264 -t 10000
```

Again, change ***** to the filename you want for your video.

The *10000* at the end of the line refers to the number of milliseconds the video recording will last for. You can change this value to alter the length of your recording (note that 1000 milliseconds = 1 second).

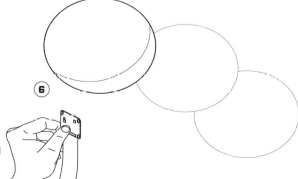

Press *Enter*. The video clip will start recording straight away. Once recording ends it will be saved to your home folder.

< 211 >

Build it! →

LEGO® Technic Case

A case is an essential accessory for a lot of projects, but rather than buy one, why not make one yourself?

MATERIALS

→ Raspberry Pi
→ LEGO Technic parts*:
→ 36 x 2M peg with friction
→ 11 x 1½M peg
→ 7 x 1M peg with knob
→ 8 x 1M peg with peg hole
→ 10 x 2M peg with friction & cross axle
→ 22 x 3M peg with friction
→ 4 x 2M cross axle extension
→ 1 x 3M beam with 4 pegs
→ 2 x 1M beam
→ 1 x 2M beam
→ 2 x 2M beam with cross hole
→ 4 x 3M beam
→ 4 x 5M beam
→ 3 x 7M beam
→ 10 x 9M beam
→ 3 x 11M beam
→ 5 x 3 x 5M 90-degree angular beam
→ 3 x 3 x 11M Panel

*note that the precise LEGO requirements will depend on how you design your case!

STATS

BUILDER	Will Freeman
TIME TO BUILD	2 hours (including design)
COST TO BUILD	Approx. $15
DIFFICULTY LEVEL	Beginner

The Project

This project uses the Technic style of LEGO to build a case to protect your Raspberry Pi. The case holds the Pi nice and snug, provides access to all its connectors, and makes it easy to combine your tiny computer with other parts, no matter whether you're working on a LEGO-specific project, or need to secure cables and fasten non-LEGO parts.

For this case, almost all of the pieces used were from a single LEGO set, and the case was built based on what was available—there's every chance you can build a case that's just as good as this with the LEGO you already own.

The Builder

As well as being one of the authors of this book, Will Freeman is a video games and technology journalist, and also writes about Technic LEGO for *Blocks* magazine.

TIPS

- Look at pictures of professionally manufactured Raspberry Pi cases to give you ideas. This case was partly inspired by the "layered" design of the popular Pibow cases.

- If you're improvising with different LEGO pieces, start from the bottom and build upward, building the case around your Raspberry Pi as you go.

- Check what cables you are using. Some USB cables need more space than others, for example, even though the connection itself is always identical.

Get the code
quartoknows.com/page/raspberry-pi

TUTORIAL

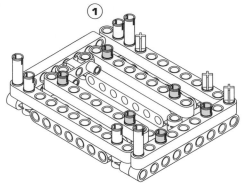

1. Build The Base

With this design, start by building a base using three 3 x 11M panels. Add a nine-hole long beam across the end of your finished base piece and then start to build up the "cradle" that will hold the Raspberry Pi in place (the small half-pegs indicated in the illustration will grip onto the Raspberry Pi).

2. Add Your Pi

Put your Raspberry Pi in place as you build upward. Start to define where the gaps to access the various ports will need to be.

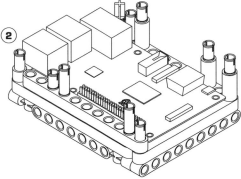

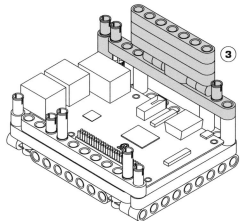

3. Add The First Sidewall

Make one of the sidewalls for the case, adding a small, hinged lid. It may help to assemble the lid section before adding it to the main case.

4. Make Some Clamps

Next, assemble the pieces that will secure your Raspberry Pi within the case. For this design we put the pieces together as shown, adding half-pegs that will rest on the top of Raspberry Pi board to hold it in place.

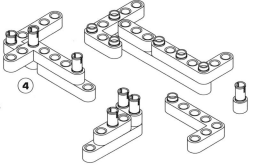

< 214 >

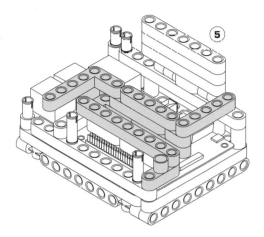

5. Lock Your Pi In Place

Connect the four pieces from the previous step together and attach them to the main case, over the top of the Raspberry Pi.

6. Add The Second Sidewall

Build up the second sidewall of the case, and the second hinged lid, which will fold down to cover the GPIO. Again, you may find it easier to assemble this section before adding it to the main case.

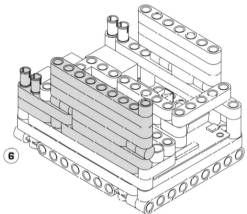

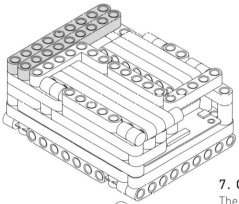

7. Close The Lid

The final section is really simple: add two nine-hole beams at the end of the case, flip the two lids down, and you're done!

< 215 >

REFERENCE

Contributor Directory

Blinking LED
Builder: Inderpreet Singh
Website: embeddedcode.wordpress.com

Shutdown Button
Builder: Inderpreet Singh
Website: embeddedcode.wordpress.com

PiNoculars
Builder: Josh Williams
Website: instructables.com/id/PiNoculars-Raspberry-Pi-Binoculars/

RoboCroc
Builder: Mark Norwood
Website: alternativepi.wordpress.com

CamTank
Builder: Chen Lu
Website: chenludesign.com

Raspberry Pi HAL 9000
Builder: Djordje Ungar
Website: instructables.com/id/RaspberryPI-HAL9000

Box Bot
Builder: Will Freeman

PIK3A Retro Gaming Table
Builder: Spanner Spencer
Website: element14.com/community/docs/DOC-80946/l/pik3a-the-raspberry-pi-3-ikea-retro-gaming-table

Micro Arcade Cabinet
Builder: Marco Tan
Website: instructables.com/member/diygizmo/

$20 Portable Games Console
Builder: Tyler Spadgenske
Website: instructables.com/id/20-Portable-Raspberry-Pi-Game-Console/

Meccano Rubik's Shrine
Builder: Wilbert Swinkels & Maxim Tsoy
Website: meccanokinematics.net

Retro Games Station
Builder: Will Freeman

Robust Minecraft® Server
Builder: Daniel Lemire
Website: lemire.me/blog/

Batinator
Builder: Martin Mander
Website: instructables.com/id/The-Raspberry-Pi-Batinator

SoilCam
Builder: Josh Williams
Website: soilcam.blogspot.com

GroveWeatherPi
Builder: John C. Shovic
Website: switchdoc.com

Astro Pi
Builder: Various
Website: astro-pi.org

PocketCluster
Builder: Sung-Taek Kim
Website: blog.pocketcluster.io

Sensor Station
Builder: Craig Hissett

Movie Player
Builder: Craig Hissett
Website: hackaday.io/project/5700-pi-video-player

Clickity-Clank: Smart Piggy Bank
Builder: Roberto Pigliacelli
Website: instructables.com/id/Clickity-Clank-Your-smart-piggy-bank

Internet Monitor
Builder: Bruce Hillsberg
Website: instructables.com/member/talk2bruce/

Internet Radio
Builder: Martin Mander
Website: instructables.com/id/1979-Bang-Olufsen-Raspberry-Pi-Internet-Radio

Coffee Roaster
Builder: Mark Sanders
Website: coffeehacks.blogspot.com

< 218 >

Cyberdeck
Builder: Jason Benson
Website: d10d3.net

Tytelli Smartphone
Builder: Tyler Spadgenske
Website: instructables.com/id/Build-Your-Own-Smartphone

Media Center
Builder: Martin Mander
Website: instructables.com/id/1981-Portable-VCR-Raspberry-PI-Media-Centre/

Lunchbox Laptop
Builder: Jason Benson
Website: d10d3.net

Yogurt Maker
Builder: Sebastian Schneckener
Website: instructables.com/id/Yoghurt-at-Home-Maker-Controlled-by-a-Raspberry-Fa/

The Internet Of LEGO®
Builder: Cory Guynn
Website: InternetOfLEGO.com

3D Scanner
Builder: Richard Garsthagen
Website: pi3dscan.com

BeetBox
Builder: Scott Garner
Website: scottmadethis.net/interactive/beetbox

Erica The Cyber Rhino
Builder: Various
Website: ericatherhino.org

Pi Camera
Builder: Henry Budden
Website: raspberrypitutorials.yolasite.com

LEGO® Technic Case
Builder: Will Freeman

Picture Credits

t = top, b = bottom, l = left, r = right, m = middle.

All illustrations by **Dario Merlo**

Alamy: Sine Chesterman 17b

Per Florian Appelgren: 176–7

Jason Benson: 158–161

Scott Garner: 26, 198–201

Richard Garsthagen:192–7

Chris Gatcum: 19ml, 19bl, 19br, 32, 34, 40–1, 86–9, 96

iStock: robtek 18 (Pi Model B), 159; janulla 19tr; wabeno 33

Peter Jonges: 90–95

Chen Lu: 58–63

Martin Mander: 106 109, 148–51, 166–71

Mark Sanders: 152–157

Shutterstock: projit48 27; Oberon 37

Raspberry Pi Foundation: 18 (with the exception of the Pi Model B), 20–1, 24, 28–31, 35–6, 120–5, 131

Rob Stanley: 9, 17t, 22–3, 25, 38, 44–5, 50–7, 64–9, 76 81, 97, 100–1, 110–9, 126–30, 136–47, 162–4, 172–3, 184–91, 208–9, 212–3, 224

Marco Tan: 82–85

Caroline Tracey: 202–7

< 219 >

Glossary

Arduino
An Arduino is one of a range of small microcontroller boards that can be used to build gadgets and devices. Raspberry Pis and Arduinos are often combined in projects together.

C
C is a programming language invented more than 40 years ago. Despite its age, this general-purpose language is still very powerful, and is installed inside all newly set up Raspberry Pis.

C++
C++ is a widely used general-purpose programming language, influenced by the C language (above). It comes installed by default on every Raspberry Pi.

Code
Code is a written language that a computer understands. It can be used to control computers, change the way they behave, create software, and much more.

Distro
A distro (short for "distribution") is a particular variation of the Linux operating system. The Raspbian operating system, for example, is a distro of Debian, which in turn is based on Linux.

Embedded technology
Embedded technology tends to refer to objects that have a technological element buried inside them. Often, this element is not obvious without taking that object apart. "Embedded systems," meanwhile, are the computer systems within devices that may also include, for example, mechanical systems.

Ethernet
Ethernet brings together a number of technologies that together allow multiple computers to be connected in a local area network, or "LAN."

GPIO
The GPIO (General Purpose Input Output) is the part of your Raspberry Pi where you can connect components, devices, and wiring. It can be rows of programmable pins sticking out of the Pi (as in the case of the Pi3), or it can be "unpopulated" (as with the Pi Zero).

GPU
A GPU (Graphics Processing Unit) is a part of a computer devoted to displaying images. GPUs are also sometimes referred to as VPUs (Visual Processing Units).

HDMI
HDMI (High-Definition Multimedia Interface) is an audio/video interface for transferring high-definition sound and images between devices: you might have used an HDMI cable to connect an HDMI TV and HDMI games console using their HDMI ports, for example. Raspberry Pis offer HDMI output.

I2C Bus
Short for Inter-Integrated Circuit. An I2C bus (also known as an IIC, I^{2}C, or Inter C bus) lets components on the same circuit board communicate with each other. In this context, a "bus" is a system for transferring data between components.

Internet of Things
The Internet of Things (or IoT) links together millions of physical devices that are connected to the Internet, and allows them to share information.

IP Address
Short for "Internet Protocol Address," this identifies individual computers when they connect to the Internet. It also lets the Internet know the approximate location of your Raspberry Pi.

Java
Like Python, Java is a popular coding language for the Raspberry Pi, which comes installed as standard.

LCD
An LCD (Liquid-Crystal Display) is a special type of flat screen display. LCD screens can be both small and affordable, and as such they are very popular with Raspberry Pi project makers.

Library
A software library is a collection of resources that certain apps and programs will make use of. These libraries can include data and pre-written code. Sometimes you might need to download a certain library onto your Pi to get something else working.

<220>

Linux
Linux is a computer operating system. The Raspberry Pi's own Raspbian operating system is based on a version of Linux.

NOOBS
NOOBS (New Out Of Box Software) is the Raspberry Pi Foundation's recommended way to install everything you need to get started with a new Raspberry Pi. Put simply, NOOBS is an operating system installer.

Maker
A person who likes to build and create their own technology, often at an amateur level. Makers typically like to improvise, teach themselves, and use affordable, everyday parts.

Operating system
An operating system enables users to interact with a computer, by providing them with tools such as home screens and cursors. It can also include basic software such as audio players, and allows applications to connect with a computer's hardware.

PCB
A PCB (Printed Circuit Board) is more commonly referred to simply as a "circuit board." They are covered in chips and other electronic components and often make up the physical base of electronic equipment, including the Raspberry Pi.

Raspberry Pi Foundation
The Raspberry Pi Foundation developed and designed the Raspberry Pi. The Foundation is also a charity dedicated to sharing the power of digital making across the world. It continues to provide free resources that teach you how to get the most from your Pi.

Raspbian
Raspbian is the standard operating system of the Raspberry Pi. You should come across it the first time you ever use a Pi.

Resistor
A commonly used component in electronics that is often employed to limit the flow of electrical current.

Ruby
Invented in Japan in 1995, Ruby is one of many programming languages that comes installed by default on newly set up Pis.

Scratch
Scratch is a coding language that is particularly good for younger and less experienced coders. It comes with every Raspberry Pi.

SOC
An SOC (System On a Chip) combines all the components that make up a computer or similar device onto a single chip. There's an SOC sitting at the center of the Raspberry Pi.

Terminal
A terminal is a tool that lets you control and navigate a computer using text entry. It's a bit like an alternative to a keyboard and mouse, and is sometimes called a "command line." The default Raspberry Pi terminal is LXTerminal.

USB
USB (Universal Serial Bus) refers to very common cables and connectors. USB can be used to link all kinds of devices. Raspberry Pis have their own USB ports. How many you have—and what type—will depend on the model of Raspberry Pi.

VNC
VNC (Virtual Network Computing) enables one computer to control another. It is often used by IT departments to remotely solve problems on different computers; to install software remotely, for example, or to run diagnostics.

< 221 >

Index

<222>

<223>

About The Authors

Kirsten Kearney has been a tech and computer games journalist for more than a decade. She began her career as a researcher and producer in broadcasting at the BBC, and has gone on to write reviews, columns, and features for many of the digital entertainment magazines and websites in the UK. She is also the author of the bestselling Minecraft® books, *Block City: How to Build Incredible Worlds in Minecraft* and *Block Wonders: How to Build Super Structures in Minecraft.*

Will Freeman is a freelance video games journalist who contributes to national newspapers, games magazines and websites, and publications written for games makers. He also serves the games industry as a researcher, event curator, script editor, awards judge, event speaker, and consultant. Will is a keen arcade enthusiast and can also be found writing about VR, board games, and LEGO®.

Acknowledgments

The authors would like to thank all of the contributors and project builders, The Raspberry Pi Foundation, and the community of Raspberry Pi makers across the world.

Kirsten would also like to thank Max Kearney (See? Told you I could do it!); Brian Reid for always being around for her; and Laura MacAllister for listening.

Will would also like to thank his wife, Keira, for all her support, and putting up with those late nights writing and tinkering; his mum, Sue, for encouraging him to pursue writing for a living; and his friend and mentor, Ronnie.

<224>